CW01662945

I*ll*th

A Journey with my younger son
through psychosis from 1999
towards Light and Life.

Maggie Durkin

To Helen
warmest wishes
Maggie

Edward Gaskell
DEVON

Edward Gaskell publishers
Riverbank Cottages
Bideford
Devon
EX39 2QR
First published 2017

ISBN 978-1-906769-78-9

Front Cover artwork:
From a painting by Ben Durkin

I*ll*th
A Journey with my younger son
through psychosis from 1999
towards Light and Life.

Maggie Durkin

Typeset, printed and bound by
Lazarus Press
Caddsdown Business Park
Bideford
Devon
EX39 3DX
www.lazaruspress.com

‘The journey through madness is essentially an individual one, we can only share part of that journey with others, most of the journey is ours and ours alone. It is within ourselves that we will find the tools, strength and skills that we require to complete this journey for it is within ourselves that the journey itself takes place.’

Ron Coleman

This book is dedicated to all who have suffered the anguish of seeing a loved one in the grip of a mental crisis and to those whose lives are changed through such.

Acknowledgements

There are so many people to thank for the existence of this book, some I cannot remember and others who may have assisted us without giving their names. To those I can only apologise and say that your input was part of Ben's recovery process for which we are very grateful.

Mary Gould now deceased, who was both Counsellor to me and a friend, trained Mike and me in a form of therapy that many years later, we used in the care of Ben. Her knowledge and wisdom was invaluable.

Dr. Tim Harlow GP now retired, who not only patiently listened to our son in his most psychotic phase but trusted us to care for Ben and gave us the support we needed.

Andrew Barkla, of The Bridge Collective C. I. C formerly Hearing Voices Network, (HVN) Exeter. His advice and encouragement offered at a critical time, meant that Ben was eventually able to become part of a team of 'experts by experience'.

Ron Coleman a voice hearer, writer and trainer, instrumental in the recovery process of many others, who has become known across the world for his many seminars regarding his experiences and coping strategies, who inspired our son to recover.

Alan Kirby writer, who gave Ben such meaningful one to one sessions, encouraging him to continue to write and put down his ideas more coherently.

Richard Skinner, Ben's most consistent private Counsellor who allowed Ben the freedom to say what he felt, without fear and offer hope where there had been none. All this was done with such gentle humour and great patience.

MIND in Exeter who assisted Ben in becoming more confident of his abilities to live an independent life by offering him a supported 'home' when he most needed it.

Some of the Mental health team that we encountered along the way did have a better understanding of how to work humanely with someone in distress of the mind, but sadly this was a rarity then and those that worked best with Ben were often the ones who were moved on or out of the system altogether.

Special recognition must be given to my closest family members, to whom I am indebted for their generous and honest input.

This book could not have been written without the help of our son Ben who has taken the opportunities given him and transformed his life from that of a victim into a victor. Ben's artwork both on the cover and throughout the book illustrates his creative energy. He is an inspiration to many others who have trodden the same very lonely path.

Our other son Sam who also has severe depression and suffers from many serious allergies along with heart trouble is very much part of this story. His continuing struggle for recognition about his own health problems whilst using his art to express his unique interpretation of the world around him.

My elder sister Doreen, who gave her time and energy freely and lovingly to care for me and Ben at a most difficult time.

The other part of our family team, my husband Mike, who despite having to work away from home was a constant support throughout the process of caring for Ben. Also, for encouraging me to write this book and help with editing.

Finally, grateful thanks to the publisher Edward Gaskell of Lazarus Press for having the courage to take a novice writer and assist her to the finish line.

Contents

Foreword

by Andrew Barkla
Bridge Collective
C. I . C Exeter

I first met Ben, Maggie and Mike when they walked into the Joan of Arc Room - a point of contact set up within Mind in Exeter and East Devon for people looking for a place to talk about and explore experiences such as hearing voices and seeing visions from a human rather than a medical point of view.

It was 2000, the early days of the Hearing Voices Movement in Devon. We had many contacts both from voice hearers and from family members and friends — often people whose loved one had many years' experience within the mental health system and who had only been offered an 'illness' interpretation of the experience.

It was refreshing to meet people who were seeking alternative approaches before much contact with mental health services. I was heartened by Maggie and Mike's belief that their son needed to be met with respect and his experiences be honoured. I remember them talking with disappointment about experiences of a 'day service' where they (and Ben) felt he and other attenders were patronised - given simplistic craft work to keep them occupied but with no opportunity to look at the experiences people were finding hard to handle.

Ben is a true philosopher. It seems his calling in life is to invite anyone open to listen into dialogue about what it is to live and experience. He often quotes Socrates as an inspiration. As in ancient Athens, so in modern England philosophers get a mixed reception, but Maggie has shown in this book how, often against adversity, Ben has been true to his path. Historically (I hope it's changing now) there used sometimes, it seemed to me, to be a feeling of three-way tension in the world of 'mental health' between 'professionals', 'carers' and 'service users' - with 'service users' treated as the 'problem' and a battle between 'professionals' and 'carers' for control over how the 'problem' should be managed.

The Hearing Voices Movement, which I was lucky enough to encounter myself and to be able to introduce Ben and his family to, was a place where that story changed. It was a community of voice hearers seeking their own paths where professionals and carers were invited to be allies. Belief in psychosis as illness that can't be cured is disempowering to everyone. The Hearing Voices Movement offered a challenge to this idea and invited everybody involved to empower themselves through building connections and communities. Nobody's view was 'right' - everyone was exploring together what could be learnt about and from experiences that had conventionally been marginalised.

In this book, Maggie describes from her perspective the journey that Ben and his family have been taking in that spirit. There are also many of Ben's own words in the book, which give a flavour of his amazing creativity, thoughtfulness and originality.

Ten years ago, Ben, I and many other committed people joined together in setting up the Bridge Collective, a social enterprise company that aims to build a community centred in Exeter based on the ideas of the Hearing Voices Movement but extending them to all experiences, feelings and beliefs that may have been labelled 'mental illness'. Ben is an active participant and volunteer in the Bridge Collective as he and Maggie describe in the book, and he has recently been elected a Director for the second time after a break. The Bridge Collective is very lucky to have Ben's unique input.

In telling her family's story, Maggie also touches thought-provokingly on a wide range of issues to do with how we as a society think about and approach experiences, feelings, and beliefs that have sometimes been labelled as 'mental illness' and the people who have been labelled in that way. I hope this book will give insight and inspiration to anyone who finds themselves travelling through this territory.

Introduction

In the beginning

I begin with Ben's first description of his state of mind as it was in 1999. He was twenty four years old, in the second semester at Lampeter University in Wales, studying Philosophy and Sociology.

This '*Ill*th' - his own word - had infiltrated his mind like some malevolent creeping catastrophe, over which he felt he had no control. He had become Psychotic and was desperate for help.

So perhaps you can understand a little of what the title of this book means and in the following pages will see how, gradually, Ben has overcome the devastating diagnosis of his condition and turned the tables on the world's perception of those who are afflicted with the many facets of mental illness.

Why, you ask has it taken so long for me to write all this down?

Well, there are several reasons, but the main one is because it is only now that I can look back over the past eighteen years more objectively.

To have written this in a state of anger and frustration at the lack of understanding we received then, would have been destructive.

I hope, despite the many difficulties and obstacles to recovery that we encountered along the way, that you will be encouraged to believe that drugs are not the complete answer, nor even the answer at all, to your own dilemma.

Also, that you seek constructive up to date advice from the more enlightened psychological approaches there are now, to mental health.

You will notice throughout that I tend to put 'client' and 'patient' in quote marks, as they are the only way that most people would understand the description of those who are at the sharp end of receiving whatever treatment is offered.

This does not mean I agree with these descriptive terms but rather that, so far, it is how they are perceived.

Our son does not feel he is a 'client' and only when visiting his GP does he consider himself a 'patient', but for many, the terms still used are the only ones that explain the recipient's status in a society which restricts their movements and choices.

Also I am more aware now, that the term 'mentally ill' is one that has been given to people who think and view life differently from what is regarded as 'normal'. But these views and perceptions in themselves are not necessarily due to an illness in the biological sense.

Many would now be very sceptical to assume that hearing voices for instance is a sign of madness, knowing how many famous people have been known to have experienced this phenomena themselves, yet not necessarily subjected to psychiatric intervention.

The first person I can think of is Samuel in the Bible who hears a voice and believes it to be Eli calling him in the night. It turns out to be God giving him a message. Joan of Arc began hearing voices when she was twelve years old and went on to successfully lead the French army into battle, only later to be denounced as a heretic. She was imprisoned, tried and condemned to be burnt at the stake. Some years later she was canonised. Mahatma Ghandi also heard a voice, which continued to speak to him right up to his death. Ghandi just accepted this phenomena as his guide.

Even the men who have formed the basis of much of our understanding of the human psyche, Sigmund Freud, the founder of Psychoanalysis and Carl Jung, a Swiss psychiatrist, heard voices.

More modern day examples are of Anthony Hopkins, Zoe Wannamaker, Lady Gaga and John Frusciante of the Red Hot Chilli Peppers, all very talented and creative people.

Trust your own instincts, remember that the person who is now so different to the one you thought you knew, still exists, but is hidden from view in this cloud of confusion and even anger. Try not to feel scared or threatened, even when the person in crisis is not able to communicate or what they say may sound alien to you.

Allow them to feel safe enough to tell you how they feel, when they are able by walking alongside and listening rather talking. Treat them with respect and gentleness. Offer some space, time and peace before asking too much of them and most important of all, continue to hope, with unconditional love.

1

Encountering I*ll*th

It was on 11th June 1999, my Birthday, that we drove to Lampeter, Wales to collect Ben for the summer recess. This was intended to be a treat, a trip to collect our son, Ben, from his University Lodgings and move him into his new 'digs' for the next term, before driving him back home to Devon, for the summer vacation.

As it had been planned a long while before, surely there was no need to change anything, just because we had not heard from him in a long while?

After all we thought, 'He is young with plenty of friends and social life there to keep him occupied, besides his studies.'

It seemed so easy to lull oneself into a sense of happy calm about the future. Ben had chosen this rather remote University and the philosophy course was just what he had wanted. There had been some initial hiccups and a certain amount of 'settling-in' to a new routine and feeling more isolated than usual. Yet, I thought with his new phone card he could always ring home, even if we could not ring him in the Halls of Residence, except in an emergency.

I kept telling myself that just not hearing from one's son could hardly be described as a crisis.

Yet the foreboding I had felt during the preceding weeks, the anxious little packet of chocolate I had sent with an encouraging letter to just 'phone us' that went unacknowledged.

This was unusual for Ben and should have sent louder alarm bells ringing.

Mike was on the crest of beginning a totally new business venture, commencing his own independent company, and with all this entailed, it took precedence over all else. Even with caring for his mother and watching over the prolonged building works on our home, the small matter of travelling to Wales seemed a long way ahead. I had so much to concentrate on that I had to leave what seemed less immediate at the time.

It was a fairly pleasant drive and I thought how lovely it would be one day if we could take our time and even stop over in a B&B on some future occasion.

Something deep in the back of my mind though, niggled me all the way there, that this might never happen. Why did I keep ignoring this feeling?

We arrived around lunch time to find Ben in his room looking simply dreadful. He was just sitting on the bed rocking to and fro and muttering softly to himself hardly noticing us. His room was in turmoil and he had not begun to pack. He looked as if he had not washed or shaved in weeks and his clothes were unkempt and quite smelly.

His Dad did his usual bright optimistic bit like, 'How are you Ben?' and 'Let's get you packed then.'

I ventured into the communal kitchen and found some other students from the same block and asked them how long he had been like this. They replied that they had not seen much of him but they *had* been quite worried, as he'd not been around and didn't seem to be eating!

I looked in the cupboard and fridge to find some food I could prepare for him, not even knowing if it was his.

I just did not care at this stage as I was in total shock. I put the kettle on for a drink, returned to his room and found him quite emotional.

He was totally incoherent, unable to put a complete sentence together, extremely distressed and afraid.

In a conversation with Ben much later, I found out he had been unable to write. He had not even been to the porter's lodge, too afraid to venture out and collect his mail.

He had stayed in his rooms a prisoner of his own fears and inability to communicate his desperate situation, totally neglected. Where were his friends I wondered; why did not someone raise some concern?

His room had to be completely cleared. So I filled several black bin bags of rubbish, and we packed his belongings, fed him and got him into the car as soon as possible. It would be a very difficult drive home.

His adjoining student neighbours, when asked, said they *were* worried about him but did not know what to do.

On arriving home he showed little interest in anything, even food, although he was clearly malnourished.

Gradually we discovered little bits more of his deteriorating condition, that he had tried to phone home, but each time I had missed the call, unaware that he had tried. Our phone then did not monitor incoming calls, unless a message was left, but he could not speak.

He had wanted to be collected earlier but just could not bring himself to telephone again. He had tried a few times in the last months but there had been no answer on the annex phone, so had given up.

We had been told not ring into him except in cases of emergency. The telephone in Halls could not accept incoming calls.

But in the light of what happened to Ben, if the crisis or emergency was undiscovered from the University end, this system simply did not work.

We believe that if he had received more support from the welfare people at the University he would never have deteriorated so badly.

Just recently he told me that he had approached his tutor at the University when he was extremely 'flakey' but felt his tutor just ignored him. It also seemed that what friends he thought he had, just vanished into the background.

In desperation, he had spoken to the resident priest of his fears and asked him for help - even exorcism. The priest responded to this obviously distressed student by giving him a blessing yet never informed the University that Ben might need urgent help.

In our current state of shock, we left all this non-responsive behaviour toward Ben's situation unchallenged, as our immediate concern was for the safety and wellbeing of our son.

Looking back I realise only too well that the University seemed to lack good communications in the campus regarding a possible student welfare crisis. I have since discovered that in the 1990s the University was experiencing its own problems regarding the future. Now it has merged with Trinity St. David, another University and on their new website they show that mental health support and counselling services are available. So hopefully the kind of situation Ben was faced with is now a thing of the past.

We never made a formal complaint as we were just far too busy dealing with his illness to try to unravel what actually happened.

I was coping with the practicalities of caring for Ben each day alone, while Mike worked in London and also I had an aged mother-in-law to look after.

Once home, we could reassure Ben he was safe, and that we would do all we could to help him through this nightmare. The first day we allowed him to sleep as long as he needed.

We tried to keep calm and made plans for a short outing to the seaside, thinking this would help Ben relax, whilst getting some sunshine and fresh air. As it was the weekend we were conscious that the the local GP surgery was not open until Monday.

I cooked some of his favourite vegan food and tried to encourage him to wash and change his clothes. On the Sunday we decided to drive down to the village of Beer on the East Devon coast.

This may all sound rather a simplistic way of doing things, but we were trying to keep our actions as normal and calm as possible to give ourselves time to asses the true situation.

Ben, though quiet, seemed to be a little more relaxed as we drove and we began to hope that in time we might unravel the cause of his distress.

He knew something was wrong with him, but was unable to put it into words, yet all seemed to be going quite well as we sat enjoying tea and coffee at a small kiosk on the beach. Time passed quickly, while we just watched the sea and Mike decided he should go and put more money in the car park meter.

Ben moved away to sit on the pebble beach, against a sea wall continuing to watch the waves, and I bought us both an ice cream.

Distracted, and enjoying my cornet, I wondered off a little way down a sloping set of steps to the sea. But on my return, I missed my footing and fell headlong towards the next step. My face hit the sharp concrete edge full on my nose, with a crack. I remembered how I just kept fighting my fear of how bad my injury might be, as I stumbled blindly up the beach.

The shock of seeing my face covered in blood as I staggered towards him prompted Ben to scream out, 'Please help my mother!' to passers-by for help.

Hearing his voice so clear and coherent, though terrified, calmed me a little, giving me the hope I needed for the long days ahead. I just prayed then that he would eventually recover.

It was a truly horrendous accident. Someone telephoned 999 for the air ambulance as the beach was difficult to cross, but it was out elsewhere. This was in the early days of this service and only one helicopter was ever available for the whole area.

My face had split open, right across my nose, and there was blood gushing out of the gaping wound. Thankfully a lady on the beach nearby knew enough first-aid to stem the flow of blood with her beach towel, and keep me calm and still until the ambulance team arrived!

I do not recall much of what happened, other than the Hospital staff asking me, after I was lifted from the ambulance, if I wanted to go straight into surgery that night or wait till morning. For some reason I felt morning would be better and was puzzled by this. They had bound up my face and stabilised me enough to get some sleep, albeit with an injection of morphine. My decision could be considered fortuitous, though, because on duty the next morning was the South African surgeon Dr. Babajous who reconstructed my face with amazing skill. Even today, I can only see a small tight line across where it was split, when I am tired or off-colour. He inserted a metal pin to repair my nose bone, whilst remaking the airways of my nose. My sight, thankfully, was restored again, once the swelling went down. This took several weeks and I could not wear my spectacles nor drive. There would be many return visits to hospital to check how my airways were working. I still have some difficulties with an occasional blocked nose and have to wear very lightweight spectacles. I would also have to take care not to allow the vunerable skin on my nose to be too exposed to the sun. A small price to pay.

For a time Mike had to balance caring for Ben, which included cooking vegan meals, with visiting me. Ben recalls that most of the meals consisted of endless baked potatoes and cheese, beans sometimes, and can no longer face a baked potato!

During these weeks Ben did not see a doctor, but just stayed quietly at home.

Looking back one could say that this accident could not have happened at a worse time, given how very distressed Ben was. Yet in some ways that is maybe what saved him from being 'sectioned' and carted off to Mental Hospital to be drugged to the eyeballs while they assessed his condition.

It allowed that very precious time for him, and us, to adjust to these new circumstances.

The memory of his voice calling for help for me will remain with me as long as I live. Although he returned to his silence for a long while after that, the sound of his concern gave me the glimmer of hope I needed, to feel able to nurse him back into life again.

Because my husband had just started a new business, he had to move up to London before I was fully recovered. I was in hospital for just a week, after this operation.

I'd requested to leave the hospital earlier than the doctors recommended, in order to get back home to be with Ben. I had to call a taxi to take me home alone as my elder sister, Doreen, unaware of how seriously I had been injured, had no way of knowing she needed to accompany me. Mike had told no one how serious the accident was. Maybe this was due to shock?

She cared for us both, until I was well enough to wear my spectacles, read and drive again. And this was a mammoth task, as Ben was only accepting organic vegan food, so most of it had to be purchased outside our village. Doreen made endless journeys with a detailed shopping list carrying heavy shopping bags from the health food shop in nearby town. A true labour of love.

Ben also began to eat his meals out of doors, so as not to contaminate our home with his 'Illth' He was not wearing shoes, for fear of hurting small creatures and his need to feel in touch with the earth. Just as well it was summer and still warm enough for all this. He wore a hat at all times for protection against his 'voices'. He constantly scribbled minute hand-written notes and long lists of what he had to do, to keep 'in the light of life'. He had an obsession with the significance of numbers and wrote them out repeatedly in notebooks.

At this stage Ben seemed afraid of all electrical equipment. The television had to be covered as Ben thought the TV screen, or any monitor screen, was Medusa's head, freezing us in our homes for ill purpose. None of his food could be put in the microwave at this time either, and he could not use the phone.

He would though, have music on all day and night. I think this helped to block the terrible voices.

Once he began to communicate in small fragments he would tell me how he wanted to stay in the 'Light and Life'.

This mantra of 'Life, Love and Light' was not only intended to drown out the voices, but to seal Ben into a safe environment. For neither Life, Love nor Light could 'possibly be bad or evil'.

For a long while he thought *he* was evil and would beg me to forgive him and not have him taken away. He feared being 'put in a home' or worse.

I assured him that there was nothing to forgive and he was always loved. Also that he would remain here, at home, as long as he needed.

Ben also had to avoid knives, for fear of what the 'voices' might manipulate him to do. So I kept the most dangerous ones safely out of sight.

I sometimes got him to use his coloured pencils and just draw what he felt like. They were wonderfully weird, expressive works which we pinned up on the walls. He would often sit out in the garden on the grass, even in the rain, gently rocking to and fro and humming to himself. I would sometimes join him and we would sit being silent together, watching the wild life and listening to the birds singing.

He said it was learning to 'Be', not to 'Do' that we all needed. I agree.

2

Earlier Family Recollections

We soon realised that managing our son's care on our own would become increasingly difficult and that he should be examined by a doctor, as soon as possible, to ascertain his condition and advise on a course of treatment.

Because of my accident, this action had been delayed, for over a month, until I was able to leave the house safely again. I made an appointment and walked down the village with Ben to see our local GP.

Dr. Harlow was very supportive and could see that although Ben would need some specialist treatment neither he, nor us, was in any particular immediate danger - the initial crisis had passed.

Due to Ben's vegan diet, the doctor prescribed liquid medication, that he felt would ease his anxieties until a further assessment could be made.

I am not sure of the exact dates here, as so much was happening, but I know it was quite some time later that contact was made with the Mental Health team in Tiverton. So Ben would have been slightly more coherent by the time he had his first meeting with a psychiatrist.

In this chapter I have tried looking back honestly over our family life, to see what might have contributed to Ben's breakdown.

My husband and I, as children, both enjoyed a typically conventional 'two married parents' and 'extended family' upbringing, which was common in the 1940s and 50s. So, when we married in 1968 and began our own family from 1972, I think we just assumed that this format would continue to offer the stability we felt essential for developing children. After all, the situation was very similar, with many aunts, uncles and grandparents. There were enjoyable family gatherings and both children were a central part of this; welcomed and loved.

Sam, was born in a small GP Maternity Unit in Portsmouth in June 1972.

Ben was born in July 1975 in Wallingford's Cottage Hospital, Berkshire. The boundaries have since changed and today Wallingford is now part of Oxfordshire.

We had not long moved to a new home in Wallingford just before Ben's birth and it is where most of his formative years took place. It was a typical, former ex-police, council house, being sold, like so many, after the reduction of the local force. It was the end of a terrace of similar properties, with a large garden, fruit trees and lots of grass. Offering plenty of outdoor space for a growing family and near to the local Primary School which they would both later attend.

When Ben was nearly a year old, in the spring of 1976, I took over the running of a small art shop from my sister-in-law in the town where we lived. Mike was an IT Research Engineer at the time and worked long hours.

Both boys would regularly go to their grandparents' house for meals and playtime when I was busy in the shop. Their grandmother, would have a special box of toys for them and plenty of paper and crayons. They loved going there and often would either help with the baking or simply play in the garden.

They attended a day nursery within the area of our local park, before going to the Primary school, just a short walk from our home.

It was after the boys began attending school in Wallingford, from 1977 that we began to notice that our family life was certainly not the norm any more. Many of our children's friends often only had a mum, or a dad, or else maybe step-parents, and not as much contact as Sam and Ben had with their extended families. Also at parties we held for them, we noticed that many children showed very little understanding of common courtesy when eating the party food or playing games.

We had always been very strict about sitting still whilst eating food and asking politely for second helpings. So even the boys were shocked by the behaviour of some of their guests!

Sam and Ben had always been quite good at sharing, especially their toys and, though not perfect by any means, rarely got out of control in public. They would have many high-spirited jousts together in the usual rough and tumble of home life.

Both children were very keen to learn to read and also to express themselves in many creative pursuits.

Yet I remember being told when attending a parents evening, that our sons were finding it hard to settle in to school life, apparently owing to the fact that they had learnt to read so early.

It was explained that I should not have allowed this to happen, as they would suffer boredom while the rest of the children caught up!

I felt this was not a very good sign, knowing what I do now about the way the education system was radically changed during the 1970s. I might have chosen to teach them at home. But I had a tendency then, to think that the professionals always knew better and did not like to challenge the *status quo*.

Both Sam and Ben showed great imagination in their schoolwork and especially in picture-making and stories. In fact Ben loved his books so much he would often be found asleep in bed surrounded by them.

Due to their early interest in music, I became keen to find a way for them to learn to play an instrument.

Electronic keyboards were in vogue at the time, so although we did not have a piano to practice on, they used a keyboard. They had some lessons with someone who had been recommended, but I later discovered she was a rather unimaginative and severely authoritarian teacher, who used a ruler as a correction tool!

This pursuit ended, not surprisingly, as neither child wished to continue.

Neither son showed much enthusiasm for sport, apart from running about with a ball in the garden or local park as, like their father, they suffered a lot from asthma and also hay fever in the summer.

But they loved dressing-up and being in plays and events in Primary School and would often play 'make believe' games of their own at home.

Having the Art Shop to run, meant that often they would both accompany me there after school. I would have some art and craft materials to keep them occupied, when the shop was busy.

I was informed that having pets to care for would help the brothers keep calm and alleviate the stress caused by bullying at school. So we got a kitten from a local farm whose cat had just a litter. The children loved to feed and play with him when they came home from school. Still unaware of the seriousness of Sam's allergies we also acquired two rabbits.

During one summer holiday time they brought home the school's two pet gerbils. They were very enthusiastic to learn more about these creatures, so we bought a book that explained how they loved to dig down and make underground nests when living in the wild. So then we purchased a secondhand fish tank to transfer them from the cramped little hamster house they arrived in. In no time at all they were digging down in the peaty soil and hiding in cardboard tubes and playing 'leap frog' so the boys told us!

Soon after this activity we found several babies curled up in a warm nest of chewed cardboard. By the time school began in September, not only did we return the gerbils given to our care, we now also acquired more animals to feed and look after. Once I even adopted a magnificent Rhode Island Red cockerel from an artist friend who kept chickens, because he was being literally 'hen pecked!' He eventually found a permanent home at Beale Park near Pangbourne.

Sam and Ben enjoyed learning about animals and caring for something smaller than themselves. These activities did seem to help them overcome some of the anxieties suffered from bullying, which in those days was seen as an accepted norm with which children would have to cope.

Their other set of grandparents lived in Eastbourne and it was always a long journey to visit them, fraught with travel sickness and boredom for young children.

But once there, they enjoyed going to the *Treasure Island Playground* on the seafront and making sandcastles and playing 'pirates'. Although my parents were much older than Mike's they loved seeing the grandchildren and my father, then in his late seventies, would often entertain Sam with some magic tricks he knew.

When I was a small child I had been mystified by this 'Eastern Prince' - my father - dressed in a turban and flowing robes, who did all manner of magic with silk handkerchiefs and colourful tubes. Making things appear or disappear. My father's family loved dressing up and when he performed for us at home, this was very special.

So Sam would want to learn how to do these amazing feats and for some while when he was young, he would have a 'box of magic' of his own.

Both children were very good at using their spare time creatively, Ben would like to go out in the garden and find flowers to make perfume! A truly messy business and not that sweet smelling, but he had fun trying!

Our family life, though very busy, was mostly a happy one, pursuing interests and hobbies, taking family holidays.

Sometimes when the weather was good and I had a free day from the shop, I would take the boys with me when I painted out doors. They would have their own sketch books and pencils and plenty to eat and drink!

Ben produced work in his primary school, that was seen as 'odd' for six year old child. I remember how broken-hearted he was when his teacher refused to put his picture up on the wall. Saying, it was, 'Because it did not look like the other children's work.' The class had been asked to paint a tree growing. So instead of working the same way as the class, where the sky was depicted as a blue line at the top, the earth at the bottom in brown and a typical 'lollipop' tree with a 'candy floss' canopy of leaves placed in the middle. Ben created his tree, growing, full of branches coming out of the trunk, with the sky wrapped around it in a rainbow full of colours (see pages 75 & 76).

The teacher did not appreciate Ben's picture for it's uniquely creative style and observational accuracy. His father and I will always treasure it. Ben also did another version, equally rejected, but both were displayed at home with pride.

Sam also, would watch carefully how I painted and would produce some lovely pictures of his own.

I remember once, when he was about eight that one of his teachers did not believe that the watercolour Sam showed him, was his own work. This was because it was unlike most children's paintings, he showed perspective and delicate looking branches against a sky that met on the horizon. I had to prove it was his own work, by showing the teacher others that he had done as well as mine, that Sam had observed while I painted. Proving that Sam had indeed followed my painting techniques and learnt from them.

I left the teacher with Sam's painting, as an example of what a child can do with a little encouragement. To this day I still regret this, as I doubt the man would have treasured and kept it as we would have done. I am very glad that I do have many others though, some framed, that show Sam's artistic progress through the years.

Primary and Junior school days ended as Sam now entered the world of Wallingford's only Secondary School.

However by the late summer of 1986, when Sam was fourteen and his brother just eleven years old, we had to move from Wallingford to a place near Romsey in Hampshire as my husband's job had changed.

Unfortunately both children suffered greatly from this disruption. Due to the timing of our move, we had to live in a B&B in Sherfield English, before we could take over our new home in West Wellow, near the New Forest, in Hampshire. Although it was a lovely place to stay and we were made very welcome, I have since learned that neither child was happy, as they were badly teased at the new school.

Living just outside the school catchment area, for this time, caused a problem with the application for school transport, so I would have to drive them each day in the car. Also it was perceived wisdom, then, that if a family was living in a B&B during term time, it usually meant they were in emergency accommodation, through some financial or domestic trouble. This was the newly introduced government method of accommodating 'problem' families, until a new home could be found! So the boys were not believed when they explained it was because the contracts on our new home had not yet been exchanged.

Several weeks followed before we were able to move into our new home in a quiet cul-de-sac off of Whinwistle Road where we lived between 1986 and 1997.

Ben, particularly, suffered from bullying at school. Being new to the area we had yet to make any friends, so for fear of reprisals we kept our concerns about the bullying to ourselves. These issues were never fully addressed and that may be why neither son seemed to progress well. School work was a constant struggle. Previously, Sam had been learning French, now in this new school, only German was taught as a foreign language, so he fell behind in this as well as other subjects.

They did both manage to obtain enough GCSE passes to gain entrance later to colleges of their choice.

Having passed through the school system Sam went onto Bournemouth & Poole Art College to study Animation, Film & Graphics in 1988. He also had some great ideas for board games and was very inventive. I am glad to say that Sam is now an accomplished artist and has sold many paintings, exhibited, and regularly teaches his skills on YouTube.

At some point, however, during our time in West Wellow Sam was introduced to cannabis by some school friends in the village and this use was passed onto Ben. It is difficult to ascertain exactly how this illegal substance was obtained and passed around. One evening, when Sam had gone out, we looked into his room to find evidence of any other drug taking. Knowing he had been put on anti-depressants we were concerned about the effects of any other substance that might be changing his behaviour. He was becoming erratic and could lose his temper very easily.

Sam had always suffered from eczema and, along with a steroid treatment for severe acne, his skin would be constantly inflamed. I think, perhaps the long term steroid treatment for his skin might have caused some of his aggression. He was also becoming extremely secretive, and it was hard to know what was really happening and why.

We found a number of cannabis plants growing in his wardrobe. Sam had rigged up some kind of light system to help them grow.

We were dumbfounded and realised that he was not only using this stuff but passing it on to others. We immediately took the plants out into the garden and destroyed them, at the same time removing the equipment.

Having discovered what was happening we tried desperately to stop it, warning Sam that he must cease this activity immediately. Sam reacted very angrily, complaining about his loss of privacy and, for the first time ever, I thought his father would hit him. Our threat of contacting the police to arrest Sam for possession, evaporated into humiliation on both sides. Sadly without being able to monitor every waking moment of their day, this became a constant battle with no winners.

Cannabis is not, in my opinion, a safe recreational drug. Its long term use especially when purchased from illegal unknown sources can have very serious consequences for anyone who might have a propensity to mental disturbances, as we have since learned.

With both sons having left school, they now spent a great deal of their spare time doing role playing games where their fertile imagination would take over and, I now believe, the group with whom they played smoked cannabis during the sessions. So the brothers began to inhabit a 'make believe' world of their own. I do not know how, as parents, we had not noticed the subtle changes in our sons habits but in hindsight much of what we might have done to stop the progression would probably have made our relationship with them much worse.

In 1989 having discovered my long lost birth family, I began making enquiries about how to trace my other relatives. As this took up many months of meetings and travel, I think this distracted both Mike and I. Although we were unaware of an increasing drug habit that was evolving within the boys' group of friends, nevertheless our family life became one of constant watchfulness and anxiety.

Ben was now attending a computer course at Southampton Technical College. He did not enjoy his time there and later transferred to South Downs College in Havant, Hampshire to pursue his interest in music. Having learnt classical guitar while still at school, with an inspiring tutor, he was now enthusiastic to study modern music.

This meant that he had to live away from home and some of his 'digs' were not very good places to be. I think he was lonely and had difficulty coping with money. This meant he had to take on night shift work to supplement his income.

He moved into a better shared house in Waterlooville Hampshire, with a much more thoughtful landlord who played a supportive role in his wellbeing.

He was at this time considered capable of achieving a place at 'Oxbridge' due to his intellectual application to study. So he moved away from music when he began to show an interest in Philosophy, Sociology and alternative Religions. I had bought him a book about Druid and Celtic beliefs, which he has said helped him in his confusion about Christianity at that time. His good grades would in time lead Ben to be accepted for a place at Lampeter University in Wales.

It was 1992 and I applied and was accepted for a year's pre-degree course, at Portsmouth Art College.

In the autumn of 1994, I had commenced my Fine Art Degree course at the Exeter campus of Plymouth University. A year later Sam moved out of Wellow to a flat we found him in Totton, Southampton. Mike and I moved from the family home near Romsey to live in Mid-Devon at the end of the same year.

So much change happening throughout the family brought new challenges.

3

Reviewing Our Family's 'Spiritual' Life During the 1970s to Early 90s

Looking back, I can see how our sons developed a certain ambivalence towards Christianity. I have tried to recall events that may have influenced how our sons present-day beliefs were formed and trusts were challenged.

Mike and I had enjoyed a very simple understanding of our faith as children growing up during the post war years of the 1950s. We attended our local Baptist Church Sunday School, Boys and Girls Brigades and later a Youth group. We received support and encouragement from both family and church members, so that our confidence in what we had been taught and how we had been shown to live, would culminate in confirming our own belief in the act of Baptism by full immersion, during our teens.

Yet, this simplistic view was challenged when a few years after our marriage, we encountered the *Charismatic Movement*.

This new aspect of worship swept across the country in the 1970s and many of the traditions we had accepted as children, changed. People were beginning to break away into groups, known then as *House Churches*.

These originally grew out of a true desire for people to allow the Holy Spirit to move and challenge the existing framework of the church, but with many people resisting such changes, a split was inevitable.

I believe the origins of this new spiritual drive were truly God-centred. But as so often happens in many faiths, new ideologies would eventually be manipulated by those desiring positions of power and leadership, thus losing the original vision.

Without going into intricate detail, I believe that the influences of the various church environments in which we found ourselves, during the boys childhood led to much confusion and uncertainty for them. The steady gentle pace of our own childhood growth was now altered to one of constant re-alignment with whatever spiritual guidance came from Elders in this type of church.

We had tried to teach our sons to ask questions about what they had been taught and not just accept everything without thoughtful consideration to its truth or relevance.

Emphasis on each person's own search for answers and reliance on being led by the Holy Spirit often led to not just one way, but many ways. Unfortunately, many times, we would find ourselves at odds with the leaders of such groups over doctrinal matters.

During the children's early years we had attended a house church based in Dorchester, not far from where we lived in Wallingford. The children here were well provided for in a caravan in the large garden. They would have Bible stories explained and draw pictures and sing songs appropriate for their age group. It was a fairly happy time for us all as we felt part of a loving community. But at some time, the accurate date I cannot remember, the church decided to move into a premises purchased in Wallingford after the elderly couple could no longer manage such gatherings in their home. There was a dynamic change to the lead structure after which a certain type of pyramidal power hierarchy, was introduced. Mike and I felt unable to stay in this group as we did not agree with the new regime. We moved the family back into a mainstream Free Church, for a short while, only to find that now this, too, had moved into a more challenging time. The Pastor no longer offered any Sunday School teaching for children, as he thought it unnecessary. So any child attending with their parents was now set adrift into the world of adult worship where they were just kept 'occupied', quietly, in a pew with a book during the services. Not much fun for two energetic boys!

When the children were around ten years and six years we eventually moved back to the Baptist Church, hoping that this would offer more stability, but this was also now in a state of flux due to the crisis of faith that the then Minister was suffering. The growth of the Holy Spirit movement was such, that although it was bringing about much change for the good, by sweeping away dusty old victorian structures, a lot of the gentle routine of weekly church going disappeared. There were many schisms within the church and often sides were taken, over doctrinal issues without those involved fully understanding the long term damage to the faith of the congregation. Often it was the children's and youth work that suffered the most from this upheaval.

Ben had been an enthusiastic reader of the Bible from an early age, so it was no surprise to us when he came to his own decision, to ask for Baptism, having believed he truly wanted to be a follower of Jesus.

It was when he was about seven years old, that along with a friend of similar age at the church, they asked to be baptised as believers.

Without any parents present, they were vigorously cross examined by the Deacons, who concluded they were too young to know what they were doing!

Ben came home, confused and in tears and this led to much heartache and feeling of rejection, which I think began the steady decline in both children's trust of adults outside of the family. I cannot tell what other damage was done, but know that Ben became less willing to share things.

By this time the children were attending Fir Tree Road Junior School and we lived fairly close to most of the places of worship available in Wallingford.

The Baptist Church organised groups to visit the Minehead Holiday camp site where 'Spring Harvest' was held.

This is a well known gathering for Christians to experience deeper teaching and have a family break at the same time.

It was also supposed to be a place of spiritual renewal. Indeed for many it was, yet both our boys found the youth teaching groups then, rather overpowering. They felt coerced by the leaders into accepting their views on bible references, especially regarding guilt, sexual attitudes and personal spiritual outlook. They did not find much opportunity to question what was being told them or challenge perceptions of anyone else's faith.

Despite all this Sam did become Baptised as a teenager, within another Evangelical House church we attended, having moved to

Hampshire. But I believe, as a result of an over critical and heavy handed stance within the church group over a friendship Sam had begun with a girl in the church, he felt alienated. Shortly after this he discarded his faith completely.

It was sad that Sam received little encouraging support within the church family, apart from us, his parents.

Ben would continue to hold his belief in God and apparently, it was the book I gave him about our Celtic origins and the Druids that kept this trust alive.

We also found that this new group in the Romsey area also had many leadership and doctrinal differences with which we could no longer agree. So we left as a family, feeling spiritually bruised.

I think just Mike and I began tentatively attending a local village church in West Wellow, for a while. But it was my introduction to Mary Gould, a most spiritually humble and gentle woman that would prove to be pivotal in our own search for renewed faith. She helped counsel me during the time I was searching for my birth family.

This is a very brief overview of this aspect of our family life, but it may offer some insight into how relationships can be put under immense strain through such seemingly simple changes.

Knowing what I do now about how these years of spiritual upheaval may have affected our children's development so crucially, I wish it had never happened this way.

The faith that I had known as a child, and the world I had known, had disappeared for good. Now the constant challenging of one's way of life and beliefs would forever be the norm.

The events that form us all as we grow, can either help or hinder our progress and this proved as much with both our sons.

I firmly believe that the way one is taught at school and how one's progress is measured can also have a lasting effect on our eventual development.

Both our sons had some very negative responses to their creative ideas and thought processes, which I think held them back from achieving their true potential.

In retrospect the house move to Hampshire happened at a phase in their lives that disjointed their courses of study and set them at odds with their peer group. Coupled with various family tensions and church problems too, I think they found life difficult and often confusing.

As with any spiritual belief system there can be many ways of interpreting what one reads or is told.

This all took place before 'social media' took a hold on daily life, but peer pressure to conform to the ever increasing experimentation of 'soft' drugs eventually led both sons down a route that would have disastrous effects on their health and progress through life.

The complexities of modern family life are ever increasing, as both parents now often have to work to secure the family's home life. Children can attend nursery schooling, sometimes at just a few months old. Less time is available for the family unit to enjoy relaxation together. Work commitments often mean that the old extended family support structures no longer exist.

It is a culmination of many factors that create tensions and problems within such a family unit and so not one particular aspect can be blamed.

So in conclusion, I feel that no one can ever claim to hold the complete answer to these varied situations we encountered. We hoped that one day we might be able to look back and realise that by endeavouring to resolve issues with each of our sons we would still retain our integrity as a family and not allow it to become disintegrated as so often happens.

Maybe the only power that truly matters, is that of unconditional love.

4

Seeking Help and Going Around in Circles

'Whilst diagnosis seems to provide an explanation for people's problems, this isn't the case. People are told they have 'schizophrenia' on the basis of their unusual thoughts, experiences, feelings & behaviour. If they then ask why they are having these unusual experiences, they are told it is because they have 'schizophrenia'. This circular argument explains nothing.'

Quoted from the HVN website

I have added the 'Going Around in Circles' to this chapter, as that is what it felt we were doing, all the time we were tracking down treatment, advice and support for our son. Many of the experiences we encountered ran concurrently and after so many years my memory for exact dates and times has faded. But I hope you will sense the same kind of confusion and anxiety about how next to proceed as you read this, because much of the time when I was caring for our son I had so many other demands on my time. Most of what happened in this chapter was over the period of one year, but it felt like a lifetime to me then!

We are eternally grateful to Dr. Tim Harlow, for having the belief and trust in us, to manage Ben's care at home. He prescribed the only vegan option of drugs available at the time and asked us to make sure that Ben took them and to return again in order to monitor his progress.

We did all that we were asked and also discussed our concerns with the doctor, that Ben was possibly undernourished on his vegan diet. We wanted to find ways of improving this, to aid his 'recovery' holistically.

I believe that diet had a strong part to play in Ben's 'Illth' and subsequent recovery.

So early on, I bought some vegan cookery books and encouraged him to choose various dishes. This was another small step forward. After a few weeks I was able to improve his daily meals sufficiently to see him gain significant weight.

Dr. Harlow gave us the address of a nutritional therapist Dr. D, who practised in Ivybridge. He believed that her approach to diet and energy fields might be able to help us restore Ben's physical health, alongside his drug treatment.

As I have no diary or calendars of this period it is hard to fix the exact dates that these actions took place.

It was probably around late summer of 1999 that I took Ben to see her with regard to his perceived allergies and to monitor his 'energy field'. She administered some supplement dietary pills to Ben and offered some holistic advice on food and lifestyle.

He also received some weeks of private manipulation and cranial massage therapy in an Exeter Clinic, which relieved some tension and gave him a sense of well being. This was fairly limited in it's lasting effects and also quite expensive.

Although well meaning, I think Ben's response to this treatment was not as positive as hoped and this also proved very expensive. Despite my letter to this doctor, written some months after and included in a later chapter we felt no satisfactory conclusions had been drawn. We abandoned this type of treatment and continued to look for other ways to improve his general health.

After the Doctor in Ivybridge and before Ben returned to eating meat and fish, I approached our GP for a possible appointment for Ben to see a NHS Dietician, due to my concerns about Ben's continued insistence on a strict vegan diet.

As despite my adding more variety now, I felt it might not be giving him a sufficiently balanced intake.

Doctor Harlow understood the situation and managed to arrange a meeting fairly quickly.

Unfortunately for Ben after only a single consultation with this local practitioner, I received a telephone call from her wondering what all the 'fuss' was about and requesting, 'what were the main constituents of his diet, as she had to draw up a plan for him?'

So, feeling slightly puzzled but hopeful of a constructive outcome, I gave her a very comprehensive list of his daily intake.

We never heard from her again. She never sent us a copy of her 'plan'.

I asked Ben if he would mind telling me what she had said to him during that one meeting, regarding his diet.

He told me that she just recommended him to eat more nuts! That says it all!

In fact looking back, Ben is sure that she was insulting him, but, like me stayed silent.

So our slow progress to find the right methods to treat him continued.

Ben expressed how he wanted to follow the Light and the Life for all time, in order to regain a sense of wellbeing in the world.

We would sometimes watch videos together, once he felt able to have the cloth removed from the TV. Surprisingly one of them was 'Shine' the story of David Helfgott the pianist who suffered a severe mental breakdown and spent many years in mental health institutions. Eventually his life is turned around by the love of someone who sees his potential and cares for him.

I wondered if this film might upset Ben, but I think because we watched it together, the difficult bits were tolerable and it finally ended in triumph of a sort. However, the sight of David rocking to and fro and muttering to himself in some deep mental agony reminded me of how we first encountered Ben in his University rooms, only a few months earlier. I can never watch this film now without returning to that moment.

Another film that gave Ben hope was The Fisher King. I also took Ben to the cinema to see Beautiful Mind and it helped him to see that he could 'solve it', his own problem, that is.

Because his father was now travelling to and from London more than staying up in a flat as before, I often had to cook a good breakfast early each Monday morning.

We had all been living in the 'annex' of the large house we had been renovating. Unfortunately Ben was having to sleep in the living room, on a sofa bed put up each night, as it only had one bedroom.

This was an added difficulty to the busy schedule of builders in and out of the main property each day. Also I had the responsibility of caring for my mother in law who we had moved to a bungalow in the village, as she was no longer able to manage entirely alone.

One morning around 6.30am after cooking the usual 'Full English' for his father before his London journey, I returned from the station to find Ben up and grilling some bacon for a sandwich. I said nothing more than, 'Good to see you cooking breakfast,' before I put the kettle on for tea.

Ben was beginning to make his own decisions!

His diet from now on returned to full meat and fish eating, with lots of fresh fruit and vegetables.

Ben was also able to play cards and some board games again. He was much slower though and the medication he had been put on had changed several times due to horrible side effects. We had constantly requested more psychological advice and less drugs.

All these seemingly small steps forward were to be just the beginning of a much more complex journey to find ways through this fog of unknowing.

Now began the treadmill of requesting help from the mental health services, through our GP.

In November of 1999, five months after he arrived home from University an appointment had been made to meet his first psychiatrist.

The meeting was attended by all three of us. It was a rather strained affair with the psychiatrist asking me what we thought 'normal' meant. An ambiguous question at the best of times. I seem to remember saying it depended on the criteria and circumstance of the situation. He just stared back at me.

He also accused me of 'colluding' with Ben on a daily basis by allowing him to make decisions and doing things with him that relieved his anxieties and that, in his opinion, was not good.

I challenged his idea of 'colluding' by saying that I was listening to Ben's perceived needs for the day and would continue to walk alongside him and go at his pace of recovery, until he felt able to walk alone again. I also believed that not all Ben had to say was mentally unstable and that we should listen to his moments of coherence, in order to establish what Ben felt he needed. That a therapy in which he could express his fears would help. So that in a healing environment and good daily routine he would slowly return to reality.

This was not well received and from then onwards, we felt a great sense of hostility towards us, from this man. The psychiatrist was puzzled that we should want to try and care for Ben ourselves. In fact, Ben believed this practitioner continued to remain annoyed with us as Ben refused to be admitted into hospital for a period of 'assessment'. He thought that he would never get out again and feared entering such a miserable place. We also knew it would mean less access to his family and familiar surroundings which had up to now had a calming and therapeutic effect on him. Ben was constantly urged to take more and stronger doses of medication, which he resisted. Suspicion built up on both sides and our request - that Ben receive psychotherapy, rather than more drugs - was never resolved.

But it was the reaction my husband and I received from Ben's psychiatrist when we said we were going to take our son on a winter cruise, that was so appalling.

He told us that we should have him put in hospital for a proper formal assessment and go away to the sun by ourselves. We knew this would have been very wrong for Ben after learning to trust us, as we knew he would feel abandoned, so we declined the demand. We also suspected that Ben would be forcibly given even stronger drugs in order to control him better within a restricted hospital environment.

Ben responded to the idea of this trip by showing a renewed interest in clothes. He stopped going barefoot and shuffling around in old jumpers. We went shopping together and bought him a completely new look. At this time he was convinced that he was a seal, so wanted everything to be in grey. He chose all his new outfits himself, during several short visits to Exeter.

Although shopping was very tiring and stressful, he began to feel so much better about himself. He now had a beautiful grey silk shirt to wear with a velvet jacket and sealskin trousers for evening wear. He began to look forward to the trip and even talk about the

Right:

Ben before the cruise

Left:

Ben on the cruise

places we would visit. At last, I could see that he was tentatively entering the real world again and not his nightmare one of blackness and fear.

The photograph taken at dinner on board, illustrates that this particular 'therapy' of ours worked!

During the cruise he stopped taking his medication, which made him feel so awful and just enjoyed relaxing in the warm sunshine on deck, in the pool and wherever we travelled.

Although it was only booked for ten days in February 2000 it was a wonderful time of much needed relaxation and fun for us all. On board we knew that Ben felt safe and we enjoyed many of the activities provided. Dressing for dinner in the evening gave Ben an opportunity to feel special. He enjoyed all the food offered and after we would play card games together in the bar area where cocktails and coffee were served.

He had a cabin to himself which was near to ours so he felt secure. We kept close company with him at his request and made sure he was never in a dangerous or threatening situation, especially when we went out for day trips to various islands and cruise stops.

We visited colourful markets, where Ben bought shorts and tops to wear. Before we left for the cruise I had difficulty persuading him to get some light weight clothes for the holiday. But here in the warm Caribbean sunshine he was happy to buy several outfits, many of which he would wear for a time, when we arrived back home.

I think that this was one of our most precious family times with Ben as we all relaxed and returned home rested.

All this took place before Ben came fully into contact with other Mental Health specialists, known as Community Psychiatric Nurses or CPN's. Most of these practitioners were fairly supportive within the limits of the care then, apart from the one psychiatrist, who disliked us intensely.

When the GP first told Ben that he would make an appointment with the Mental Health team. Ben asked if he could talk to a man. So they sent a young woman!

When she arrived she decided that a good 'family' chat would help. But as Mike was away and there was only me, it hardly seemed appropriate.

Ben requested a private meeting, so this should have been paramount. So much for listening to the client's needs back then!

I doubted if any case notes had been made or even read before her visit, as she seemed to have little or no comprehension of just how psychotic he was.

By now, Ben had regained his speech and was conversing quite well. But it was only when he began talking about 'mother spider' and how he could feel the cosmic energies from the television that she became visibly anxious and, Ben felt, rather patronising.

This reaction upset him, and he vowed he would have nothing more to do with the mental health system.

It was only by a great deal of gentle coaxing that I managed to persuade him to give it another try. Even I could see that he would need the support of mental health practitioners to secure benefits and later, perhaps, work. Something we could not do alone.

The next contact was made by a male CPN and although he arrived in a suit which Ben found over formal, he very gradually learnt to trust him. He was considerably more enlightened and was instrumental in getting the only respite care that Ben has ever received. (Which, by the way, sadly, turned into a complete fiasco and I have written about it in Chapter 8)

He also helped Ben get his first benefits through and organised social activities to help integrate him into a more structured weekly regime.

Ben began attending a small writers group in the village for mental health 'clients'. It seemed quite good at first, along with a 'craft' meeting in the same venue, until Ben's work was criticised for being too peculiar, and non-conformist.

He is highly sensitive to atmosphere and believed that they were deliberately trying to undermine him and mock his creativity.

He also told me that the craft work was very patronising, not really taking any account of what the recipient wanted or needed. For instance the Mother's Day card they made him produce was nothing like the one he would have designed and to top it all had a pink pig stuck onto the front! Both he and I found this quite offensive, and certainly not suitable to give on such an occasion.

So together we delighted in throwing it away. Ben's artwork was being rejected again, because it was 'odd'. Memories from school, came flooding back. But I continued to encourage him to write and draw at home, whatever he felt like and keep it for himself. We stuck up loads of his work all over the place. I purchased several note books and pens for him to write anything he wished, without having to show anyone. This proved a good decision, as he still enjoys putting his ideas down and keeping records. Taking photos from interesting and unusual viewpoints is another creative area he has tried since.

He went to the writers' group for a few more sessions, just to see if things changed, but decided not to continue, as he did not feel it suited his needs.

Another opportunity for Ben to get out, become more independent and hopefully make friends, came when he obtained a place at 'The Old Bakery' in Tiverton. This was a day care respite centre, mainly for people with many types of mental health conditions which also included severe learning difficulties and developmental disorders. This was also supposed to be a place to help and support Ben. They had their own monthly magazine 'Stepping Stones News' which encouraged people to contribute. Ben wrote in one edition a moving account of an experience he had. 'Confessions of a Manimal' (see Chapter 7 'Ben's own words') which I believe contained clues regarding his later re-entry to Light and Life.

Yet because of a badly managed dispute with the staff, this place eventually became a no-go area for him.

Ben still wanted some spiritual guidance and support and asked me if the local vicar would be willing to meet him. I made some enquiries and was slightly perplexed by the response, which seemed rather cool considering that Mike and I were regular members of this church.

However, one Sunday Ben plucked up enough courage to come along with us to the morning worship. As Ben very tentatively entered the church, a man stepped forward and quietly, but firmly asked him to either remove his hat or himself.

I had hoped, in this enlightened age, knowing there was a troubled soul wishing to join the congregation, that the normal christian acceptance would be welcoming. Yet despite our being quite open with the local christian community about our son's mental condition, it seems this was not fully understood.

Ben removed himself silently and I left with him in utter amazement. We took solace in our home and garden close by.

You may consider this an insignificant action and hardly one that merits a mention. However it had added to the earlier rejection of Ben's childhood request for Baptism that was also turned down because they deemed him to be too young to know what he was doing. Now here he was a man, frightened and confused who was viewed too crazy to be socially acceptable in polite society. He was too scary for sane folk to encounter alone and worse of all he was manipulative. 'All schizophrenics are, you know,' I was later told by the vicar.

Ben wore his hat to protect his head from the voices; and he wore no shoes to protect the earth from his heavy tread in fear he should kill something. He walked in constant dread of who or what he had become and where he might end.

I still fail to see the vicar's reasoning not to minister the peace that Ben so needed. I may have long forgiven this act of insensitive spiritual ignorance knowing that our son has since talked socially with this man and was able to explain his position more positively since his recovery. Yet the long term repercussions of such attitudes is sadly still at work today in society. Non acceptance of damaged, vulnerable and frightened people wishing to enter places of historical 'sanctuary' like churches, can affect the spiritual growth within the church.

So from the terrified priest in Wales, who could not bring himself to offer more than a quick blessing, to the University authorities who would rather turn a 'blind eye' to the suffering of one of their students, the world still has difficulty offering help to those in mental turmoil.

All that Ben wanted was an acceptance of his need to ask for forgiveness and seek some peace for his anxious mind in constant turmoil. To be given reassurance that he was not a wild beast or evil, but a soul who needed protection. Just a moment within that service where the peace is offered each to each, Ben may have felt accepted once more by the wider community.

As it was he would have to endure the situation of being 'safe' at home, yet a prisoner still, of all his fears.

I never entered a church to worship again until 2015, when the welcome was genuine and I knew the healing process, for me at least, could begin.

Ben's CPN was very supportive and most of all reliable and consistent in his visits, in fact one of the best Ben ever had. He arranged for Ben to have his first appointment with a Psychologist in Tiverton in September 2000. He progressed really well with this man and we saw a visible change in Ben's disposition. He became more upbeat and was full of hope. But like so many treatments that were offered reluctantly they were quickly withdrawn once any benefit was noticed. When he lost his support psychologist it was a terrible blow to Ben. The doctor moved on to Plymouth and we were told that he would not have been entitled to any more sessions at that stage. By December 2000 he had seen the Psychologist just five times so I guess this was his allotted quota! Just as he was feeling upbeat, he was put down again. There followed quite a difficult time with Ben growing more restless and wanting get things moving.

We also often had to assist Ben with his financial muddles. Forms for application for benefits were a nightmare to complete as there where so many questions that could be answered wrongly if one did not read through carefully.

During the summer while waiting for his first Psychologist appointment we had discovered the Hearing Voices group in Exeter, known as The Joan of Arc Room. I really cannot remember who had told us about this group, but am so thankful that we made contact.

We made the journey to the Joan of Arc room in Exeter with some trepidation as we were rather nervous about trying yet another kind of help group when so many had proved to be completely useless due to lack of vision or understanding. Our fears though on entering this welcoming place were proved totally unfounded. It was so lovely to just be accepted and for Ben to be given some time to explain how he felt.

I have included a letter in the correspondence chapter that I sent some time later expressing how much we had all appreciated the welcome they gave.

Ben stayed with this group through its transition to the Bridge Collective C.I.C. (Community Interest Company) which now includes more than just voice-hearers in its meetings. Having attended several meetings in the Joan of Arc room, we heard about a seminar that was taking place in Gloucestershire on coping with voices. Ron Coleman had been a voice hearer with a diagnosis of schizophrenia and yet had written a book about his 'recovery'. We went to the seminar in October 2000 and were overwhelmed at being informed that current treatment for voice-hearing consisted only of prescribing dangerous neuroleptic drugs. This was a major breakthrough. We had despaired of finding intelligent non-critical and supportive encouragement for our son but now, at last, things seemed to be moving in the right direction. We were meeting people who had recovered sufficiently to have fulfilling and meaningful lives.

It has not been easy taking time out to transport Ben to all the various places and activities which we felt would revitalise him, but we had made a promise to see it through and he has acknowledged that we have always acted in his best interests.

He started making friends locally in the pub and around the streets in the village where he lived with us. Somehow in his mind he was trying to reach out to others, who might be having problems like himself, to see if he could help by starting a small local group.

This brought its own problems, with people not understanding his motives. We saw quite clearly that he was lonely and that he was looking for others nearer his age group with whom he could engage.

Ben began to go downhill again. It was late autumn and throughout the long summer months, he had been hanging around in the village square with youngsters. Eventually someone disliked his actions and beat him up. During this time he went through a 'Ghandi' period where he felt compelled to live in poverty and own less belongings. Ben tells me that an insistent voice saying 'buy and sell comes from hell, possessions are possession,' was constantly bombarding him at this time.

He gave away nearly all his book collection, most of his CDs and a large quantity of videos. He also gave away a Play Station his brother had lent him. All this caused a tremendous strain upon the family and we were by now at breaking point, having no respite from caring for him.

But we are not quitters, so we began to discuss with his CPN the possibility of Ben going into supported accommodation outside the village. Perhaps he might meet more people nearer to his own age and have greater external support. I also wrote a letter, dated October 2001 requesting urgent assistance, to a Psychologist Ben had met earlier. (see Chapter 9)

Ben did receive a kind of response when his CPN at the time arranged for a placement for Ben in a Residential unit in Tiverton.

A fresh start was what was needed now. We hoped that this might help him regain his confidence.

The author with her sons Ben, left, and Sam, right. The photo was taken in her old Devon garden.

5

Moving Out and Moving On

The residential place which Ben's CPN had managed to secure was a unit designed to assist a more independent life style for people with various mental health problems.

This enabled us to resolve the problem Ben was enduring with wrong perceptions of his actions in the local community. It was to be the beginning of Ben living a more independent if rather precarious life away from his family. But it did not address the issue of the entitlement to therapeutic treatment we knew he was owed.

He was less than enthusiastic about the move at the time but realised it was his best chance of becoming independent. After all this was what we had been working towards.

At Riverside, in Tiverton, Ben made new friends and became an active member of the house committee where suggestions by the tenants could be raised. He even wrote out a formula for improving the daily structure there, once he felt settled. He enjoyed being in a small community and generally felt well supported by the staff apart from the time when, due to a new Government initiative called 'Supporting People', crucial emotional support was withdrawn. The theory, it was claimed, was that the staff did not become too closely involved with 'clients'. We still believe it was really a cost cutting procedure as all night-time assistance was withdrawn. This had a devastating effect on Ben's confidence, as often it was at night that things in the house became difficult with other occupants; leaving Ben to feel a responsibility to intervene when problems arose; a responsibility that was not his, and which often put him in opposition to the staff.

However, when it was time for him to move on, they held a party for him and he has returned to several of their social events since moving to Exeter. Two of his friends from Riverside also began visiting him when he moved to Exeter.

At the beginning of May 2002, Ben went to live in a supported 'hostel' in Magdalen Street, Exeter. He now had a new doctor and care team. We had the impression that there was a more co-ordinated approach to care in Exeter. Also it was sufficiently distant from our home for him to gain a greater sense of independence. He still battled with the benefits agencies and the uphill struggle with his mental difficulties.

The large amount of complex benefit forms were extremely stressful for Ben as he battled to understand what the answers should be. Problems could arise if there were any mistakes, so keeping records and being aware of subtle changes was essential in order for Ben to be assessed correctly for that to which he was entitled.

These forms may have improved slightly now, but are always a challenge.

He felt, quite rightly, that since the summer of 1999 he had progressed. He had worked hard to achieve a worthwhile role in society and held a more realistic understanding of 'who' rather than 'what' he is. The Joan of Arc group in Exeter was now his regular place of growth and encouragement.

However, Ben had a tendency to seem more upbeat than he was probably feeling. This led to confusion with anyone treating him. If he feels hopeless and unable to explain his situation he begins to deteriorate. He needed encouragement, respect and opportunities to improve, not just to be dosed with drugs to douse the effects of psychosis.

The 'hostel' style accommodation seemed to be going well at first but then a worrying set of events culminating with Ben's mental deterioration proved that this place was not as safe for him as we had been led to believe.

He told us that non-residents would enter late at night and that the rooms were not secure. He had some food stolen, which on his low income he could ill afford to lose. He said the place felt threatening and staff were not available when problems arose.

We started to look for other places he might live. I even tried the YMCA only to be informed by a young man interviewing us that they did not take people with mental health problems as it might pollute the other residents! An extraordinary statement given it was supposed to be based on Christian ethics and not the kind of welcome expected: perhaps he had not received his full training in public relations!

I had heard that MIND in Exeter sometimes offered accommodation, if they had space. So I telephoned them seeking an interview after contacting Ben's none too enthusiastic new CPN. She felt I was going over her head, but we were desperate to get Ben out of the 'hostel' type setting in which he felt unsafe.

Her response was that it was an unnecessary fuss and could be resolved. The following is part of the letter I wrote to her explaining Ben's difficulties.

> 'He still has a way of masking his problems with outward displays of cheerfulness and a seemingly positive attitude, which can often be mistaken for 'being together,' when in fact the opposite is the case.
>
> It takes quite a bit of coaxing sometimes to realise that he is having difficulty coping. For example, during his stay with us at Christmas, we discovered that the growing collection of music CDs that he said he was replacing after his last 'Give away' episode, had in fact almost gone. Just four left.
>
> He is still having problems with obsessional tendencies, managing his daily affairs, and keeping his own environment clean and in order. He has given us his paperwork dealing with his finances and social security /benefits as he cannot cope with keeping them in order. He frequently mislays important documents which causes serious problems. We have had to write to the Student loans company because he had received a letter from them a long while ago regarding payment and it became an urgent matter. We have had to book an appointment with his Bank manager, change his bank account to one that limits his withdrawals and prevents him becoming overdrawn. We have helped him to pay off and close his credit card account. He is now continuing to put by a little each week into my account to pay off his overdraft.

> He arrived to us for his Christmas stay, quite withdrawn and grubby. He brought with him a large bag of washing. He slept fitfully and seemed to be having a great many nightmares at first. He is chain smoking again. We had long talks with him, and found out that he feels very insecure at Magdalen Street. He says that people are breaking-in and walking about in the house at night. He keeps his door locked always. This may be fact or perceived, whichever the case his anxiety levels visibly rose on his return last weekend. We feel that his removal to a more secure, supported accommodation be given top priority.

Thankfully and much to the relief of Ben, after some careful negotiation between ourselves, the current CPN and the MIND team, we managed to secure Ben a place in one of MIND's fully supported houses. So, in about May 2003, Ben moved to his new 'home': a shared house in Alphington Road. Not the quietest of places, situated as it was on one of Exeter's busiest roads, but one where he was given a light, airy room and made to feel part of a small community again!

Ben was very happy and although he had to have a new GP and cope with yet another change in his medication, he felt encouraged by the friendly feeling in the house: all occupants having household duties to fulfil each week. This gave him more structure and security. He began taking more interest in communal activities.

All the residents in this house were well supported by MIND and Ben began to feel more in control of his life. He was making more friends, getting out and socialising. He often cooked main meals to share with the others and this became quite an enjoyable event. But his money worries still dogged him and he was drinking too much. Often the only place open in the evenings for Ben to meet people was the pub. This was not a very safe or secure environment and his voices would trouble him even more when influenced by alcohol along with his neuroleptics. So we would still need to visit Ben as often as we could and take him out to lunch when he was suffering from these 'ups and downs' sessions. We would try to help by taking him shopping and generally sorting out any money worries without interfering too much with his new routine. He was still waiting to see a psychologist.

We had to make further appointments with Richard Skinner, his private counsellor, due to another recent crisis in Ben's recovery.

He had taken an overdose of his neuroleptics when feeling desperate for some change in circumstances. This would not have killed him, but it was not a very good thing for his health. We were very anxious that this should not happen again, due to lack of mental welfare.

We continued to hope that effective cognitive therapy would take precedence over the constantly changing chemical cocktails being offered.

Part of a statement written by me, in support of Ben follows to illustrate our continual need to constantly update facts, in order to keep our records straight and to help us identify circumstances that may have changed or were going seriously awry.

Mostly it was just a general slog we seemed to keep repeating, asking for more support, before another crisis occurred.

> October 30th 2003
>
> Ben has now been living in Alphington Road for about six months. After some initial problems with the existing residents, things have now settled down fairly well and he seems to be adjusting reasonably well to domestic life. He enjoys the company that is there and generally views this place as his 'home'. He still find it difficult to manage his money and often goes on a wild spending spree regretting it later. To combat this continuing problem he leaves a regular amount of cash with the office to keep for his weekly necessity shopping. This has worked quite well so far but does still leave him relying on others to keep his finances under control.
>
> All the staff who work at 88 have been very supportive of Ben and get on well with him. They monitor the state of his room regularly and encourage him to keep it in good order. He has some very nice furniture and soft furnishings with help to encourage his self awareness and esteem.
>
> The 'house' members go out roughly once a month on a social outing to keep them all in touch with each other and for their general well being and enjoyment. Ben likes this aspect of living here as he does not feel so isolated as when living at Magdalen Street.

He does not attend the Hearing Voices group so much now and that is a pity as this is another very supportive group for him where he was beginning to feel that he also had a contribution to make to society in general. It may have been, he felt too much pressure regarding the music workshop.

During these times he would talk to us about what he felt was really going on in his life. We were glad that his honesty about his problems kept us aware of how vulnerable he still was.

This did not prepare us though, for a new situation in which he found himself.

A young woman had been encouraged to make friends with Ben at one of MIND's meeting places and they very soon became romantically involved. So much so that Ben was persuaded to move into a privately tenanted two bedroomed flat away from the MIND house in early December 2006. We could see that he was determined to move on with his life, so helped to secure the new home and organise the tenancy agreement and much of the paperwork that goes with changing address from supported accommodation to a private landlord's flat.

All seemed to be going well: the young woman 'A', seemed outgoing and friendly and very excited to be moving in with Ben. I even took her out shopping with me to get to know her a little better. She was full of fun and loved buying clothes and enjoyed all the new things needed for setting up a home together.

By Christmas, with decorations up and festive mood in the air, we were beginning to notice some subtle changes in their relationship. Although the first impression was one of brightness, I noticed a change in Ben, especially when he came to spend Christmas with us and 'A' went to her parents. He spoke of how her mood would change suddenly, so that she became uncommunicative or even angry for no apparent reason. He was confused by her outbursts and upset that he could not seem to please her.

Things began to fall apart between them and it was fairly soon we realised that this young woman may be bi-polar (it was still known as manic depressive then). Ben thinks she may also have been schizoaffective with a possible borderline personality disorder.

Apparently she had not been taking her medication and this made her suffering worse. Ben did his best to try and keep things calm between them, but he was trying to cope with his voices shouting at him accusingly. They were both now in serious need of help.

There was such a commotion one day that the neighbours called the police and 'A' was taken to the local mental hospital. Once stabilised she returned to the flat, but against the wishes of the mental health team.

When they realised she had absconded they rushed across to Ben's flat and proceeded to keep watch outside, as health and safety regulations would not allow direct contact with a 'violent' patient.

I was inside the flat with 'A', calming her down, drinking coffee and trying to persuade her to return with me. We eventually did this and what I saw in the hospital later, regarding the methods they used when responding to her fearfulness, I will never forget. It was awful and humiliating.

Eventually she returned to the flat but after only a few days, she suffered another unfortunate outburst. The police once more intervened and this frightened young woman was tasered and dragged off to a secure hospital in Bodmin.

Ben was desperate to help her, as he could see that all this outrage was caused by fear. Despite his problems of travelling to unknown places alone, he made the journey all the way to Bodmin Hospital to visit 'A'. She wanted him to become her next of kin, if anything should happen to her, but thankfully he was able to realise that this was not a good idea for either of them and declined.

Unfortunately 'A' would become further depressed and agitated and eventually ended up in Broadmoor Hospital. Such a sad ending to what might have been a happier existence for them both, if given more support.

Ben lost contact with her after exchanging a few letters.

He has lived in this flat ever since and is now fairly content with his quieter life. But as I write, his mental health support from the MIND team has been withdrawn due to funding cuts. The reason given is that he now needs less support.

It is so easy to look at Ben and see a perfectly well behaved man in his forties, living in a general muddle at home but cooking reasonable meals for himself and sometimes his friends. All so very 'normal' it would seem.

But though on the lowest dose of Quetiapine that he dare take, he is still hounded constantly by negative voices; voices he struggles to hold in check. He avoids large crowds of people, especially ones he does not know personally, as the amount of information they give off is too overwhelming for him to assimilate. Travelling on public transport is difficult and stressful. The urge to jump off a platform when on the railway is intense, walking along a busy street to the shops without a companion can result in a similar urge to dart into the traffic to escape.

None of these daily symptoms of anxiety seem to be enough to warrant psychological support. The constant over reliance on prescribing ever stronger drugs, does not alleviate these problems, in fact it is well recorded that they can make them worse. Do the government really think that just prescribing drugs and leaving vulnerable people to manage 'in the community' is the proper way to treat anyone?

Our communities do not work the same way as the old fashioned villages or rows of tenement houses did in the 1940s. Most people now, do not want to know that they live next door to a schizophrenic or someone with a personality disorder, in case they become dangerous!

So these vulnerable folk are left to manage as best they can anonymously, with what little voluntary support is offered. Even today young and old alike are often sent miles away from their family and friends if they are unfortunate to 'fall' ill enough to need a hospital bed.

This leads to more and more feelings of despair and isolation.

Whenever are we going to learn in this country that it is not rocket science to really care for people kindly and with dignity?

All is needed is some joined-up thinking and a will to follow some of the best examples in the world of real working community care.

6

Walk the Walk, Talk the Talk

'One ounce of practice is worth more than tons of preaching'
Mahatma Ghandi

What gave us the arrogance to think we were capable of caring for a severely disturbed, mentally ill son? We certainly did not feel arrogant, but we did know how important it was to give Ben as much opportunity as possible to receive appropriate and timely help for his immediate needs.

Mike and I had attended a counselling training course, in the 1980s, that was based on listening to the person requiring help and gently assisting them to form their own conclusions about how they felt and what could possibly remedy a change. Little did we realise just how just how utterly essential this training would become ten years later.

We believed that this type of counselling could be applied to Ben's situation as we tried to unravel the turmoil in which he was enveloped.

Due to the fact that our two years' training was never accredited in official terms of counselling, we could not use it in any public way or set up as private counsellors.

Yet we always had a positive feeling that the time spent doing this very gentle 'listening' type of counselling might one day prove useful.

Today the Bridge Pastoral Foundation, as it is now known, still offers seminars to many professional groups and a certificate is given, on request, to those who attend the full course of seminars.

We were introduced to The Clinical Theology Association, as it was first known, after an encounter with a most interesting and amazing woman who was paralysed from the neck down.

Mary Gould had contracted polio whilst in her second year at Nottingham University.

After the initial shock of her extremely debilitating paralysis and a prolonged time in an 'iron lung', as they were known in the 1950s, Mary was eventually able to attend various treatments in a variety of hospitals which would help her to breathe outside this huge machine. Still needing assisted care she eventually managed to return to her studies and obtain an excellent degree, which opened the door for a career in teaching. Later she began to work in the area of counselling within a college environment.

She may have been in a wheelchair and have difficulty breathing, only able to use her mouth as the result of Polio, but she was to prove more 'free' than anyone I had ever met before.

The type of counselling she introduced us to was based on Jungian theories, rather than Freudian ideology, along with a deep acknowledgement of christian principles. It was not the type that just quoted biblical texts at someone until they caved in and announced they were saved: I'd had an experience of that sort many years before.

This method was one of true acceptance of the person in whatever condition they were.

Listening patiently as they explained how they felt and allowing them to find their own way through the problem.

Respecting their views and ideas as they begin to discover new ways to view the situation in which they found themselves, before beginning to take control again of their own future.

What we felt was so important was that nowhere was any remark made about one's spiritual beliefs or sexual orientation. Accepting someone as they are offers them to time to proceed at their own pace and just 'be' where they can feel they have accomplished new personal growth. Working alongside people is preferable than counselling to them.

This is a very shortened and simplistic explanation to a much more complex set of actions between the client and counsellor, but as you can see it has a strong basis in what most people now know now as 'Talking Therapy'. The following is the mission statement of BPF (Bridge Pastoral Foundation):

> Founded on the groundbreaking insights of Dr Frank Lake, BPF exists to bring a theological dimension into training for psychotherapy, counselling and related caring professions, especially those who work with people suffering from spiritual and emotional distress. Founded in 1962 as the Clinical Theology Association, we run a variety of courses, conferences and care networks for those working full-time in these areas, or as part of a wider responsibility.
>
> A key element in our approach is that, in order to care for others, we must first understand ourselves; much of our training, which is highly experiential, focuses on this.
>
> <u>Our Vision</u>
> BPF'S vision is of a future where all people, irrespective of their belief or religion, are given opportunities for personal growth and training based on spirituality and psychotherapy, enabling them to accompany in a supportive manner, those who are struggling with emotional distress.
>
> <u>Our Values</u>
> BPF believes in the uniqueness and value of each human being and promotes a holistic approach to pastoral care, professional counselling and psychotherapy training (encompassing body, mind, emotion and spirit). We offer a dynamic model characterised by:
>
> the unconditional acceptance of each person;
> staying with people in their struggle 'to be';
> Working at the interface of spirituality and psychotherapy.
>
> <u>Who can benefit from the BPF approach?</u>
> People in the caring professions (or those who simply want to help others) often find themselves lacking the resources they need to do the job properly.
>
> Psychotherapists, counsellors, doctors, nurses, ministers, pastors, carers and social workers are among those professions which have utilised our techniques and insights. Although the Christian faith underpins all that we do, we welcome people from any faith or none'.

CBT (Cognitive Behavioural Therapy) is a different kind of talking therapy which is highly structured to a set of fixed criteria and may not always be suitable for certain types of mental disorders. This is usually the only one that is offered to NHS patients and has an extremely long waiting list.

So, when seeing how little Ben was first able to communicate, we patiently waited until he felt able to use whatever methods suited him best. He was in a total state of confusion and seemingly unaware of day to day reality as we understand it.

Minute handwriting would appear on small bits of paper with bewilderingly long lists of names and numbers, all deeply significant to him. This was all he could produce for several weeks, while his mind was bombarded with so many voices.

We accepted these ways of 'speaking' and allowed him to feel that these written fragments had the same enormous significance to us, as they seemed to have with him. We continued to treat them with respect, storing them in a safe place until he was able to speak coherently, some months later, and could decide for himself whether to keep them.

Allowing him the space and freedom to feel safe, in as peaceful surroundings that could be offered during major building and renovation work on our main house, we tried to plan the way ahead. I had felt strongly about the need for good nourishing food, which was both interesting and enjoyable, to build up his run down system.

Not an easy task, when at this time he was a strict vegan and the lack of good 'health food' shops nearby proved another obstacle to overcome.

This initial approach to Ben's condition was, apparently the best method we could have used.

I have now discovered a similar one, that has become known as the Soteria Method of treatment.

'Soteria,' briefly, is known as the greek goddess of spirit, safety, deliverance and preservation from harm.

A community was set up as a research project in San Jose, California in 1971 by a psychologist Loren Mosher. This was a place where patients could experience a place of loving acceptance, good food and understanding rather than the drugs and clinical atmosphere of psychiatric wards based on the medical model of control by doctors who would attempt to 'treat' and 'cure' the perceived 'illness' often by force and coercion.

In this atmosphere of tolerance and the non labelling of occupants, it was hoped that the primary focus could be on development, learning, and growth. That this should be worked through with those who entered

Members of staff at the house were encouraged to treat residents as peers and to share household chores. Any visitor would find it hard to distinguish the difference from those being treated to those assisting, as no uniforms, no badges or medical style regalia were worn. The programme was designed to create a quiet, calming environment that respected and tolerated individual differences and autonomy. There was also an ethos of shared responsibility for the running of the house and playing a part in a mutually supportive community, with the distinction between experts and non-experts downplayed (similar to therapeutic communities). Psychotropic medication, including anti-psychotics, were not completely rejected and were used in some circumstances. The staff in the Soteria House were significantly more intuitive, insightful and flexible with a greater tolerance of altered states of consciousness, compared to staff in other psychiatric services. The history is worth reading.

In the UK now, they state:

> 'We are a network of people promoting the development of drug-free and minimum medication, therapeutic environments for people experiencing *psychosis* or extreme states. We are part of an international movement of service users, survivors, activists, carers and professionals fighting for more humane, non-coercive mental health services.'

There is another strategy being used to assist those in the grip of serious mental crisis, called the 'Open Dialogue'.

This approach has been in used in Finland for several years and is at last beginning to be recognised as a better way of helping people than the all too prevalent drug and psychiatric control centred clinical methods.

Again, all this was unknown to us at the time of our initial caring for our son or we would have sought to access this type of service.

The focus is primarily on the person who needs help. The idea, very simplified, is to offer an opportunity in a safe and calm environment for there to be a two-way conversation, or in the event of loss of spoken communication, a time of sitting with someone to allow flow of thought to develop gradually. This would not necessarily be with a medical person but more likely someone who has possibly experienced similar trauma and has been trained to apply their own understanding to the needs of others.

So in those first few weeks when I was still unable to get about much after my accident, Ben and I would just sit quietly listening to his music. Sometimes he would be busy writing or simply staring into space, barely functioning in the day to day events around him.

This was our 'open dialogue' I guess, and one which I believe benefited us both.

Very gradually he would engage in small ways around the home, especially in preparing vegan meals with me from the many recipe books I had collected. He needed constant encouragement to wash and change his clothes.

Days would go by when nothing seemed to be happening and with so much responsibility caring for my aged mother-in-law as well as overseeing the building work on our house, I could easily be lulled into a false sense of security. Planning the future was difficult as Mike was still working away in London, only returning at weekends, so it was mainly just myself who had the job of finding ways to encourage Ben forward.

Often, on going out for the day, we would get to the local place of interest only for Ben to feel too insecure to get out of the car and enter. But one day we made it all the way to Dartmoor! He got out of the car striding along ahead, with his hat firmly on and of course, by this time wearing shoes. However he did not want to talk, which I found disconcerting: but had to accept that for Ben, just at that time it was about 'being' not 'doing'. I just had to let him be.

As Ben became more relaxed about travelling, I would drive to Totnes and there we would have a veggie lunch. This was a town where Ben felt very 'at home'. Probably as there are so many esoteric and interesting bookshops in which he would happily browse for hours. The atmosphere there lent itself to his 'cosmic aura' at the time.

Also we would visit places like Glastonbury and climb up the hill to stand silently in the ruined tower. We had visited there before when he stayed in the cottage I had in Cullompton whilst I was doing my art Degree.

These outings had a very calming effect on us both and were some of our happiest moments.

Often I would find Ben just rocking to and fro listening to the same piece of music over and over.

He liked Beth Orton and had one piece of hers 'She Cries Your Name' which he played repeatedly. When I hear it today, I still remember the deep feeling of anguish I felt then. He would fill tape upon tape, of recordings from the long lists he played. Apparently he was trying to send messages to us via his music choices.

Many note books of spidery writing would be filled, letter after letter written and rewritten, but never posted.

This was how he spent his first months until treatment from the local mental health team kicked into action. Observing these activities would give me the necessary insight needed for aiding Ben's progress toward recovery.

Another way in which I could interact with Ben's perception of his future plan came when he told us he wanted to go away and learn to live next to nature. He wanted to find a place he could live safely in woodland.

I could see that he was far from capable of doing this but as he became agitated about wanting to get away, I made a plan with him suggesting that we should buy things that he would need, like maps, a compass and waterproof clothing. We also agreed that plates, pots, pans, and utensils were essential for cooking out of doors.

I found a list he had written in preparation:

<u>Home</u>

Treehouse

1. Should be like a nest
2. Made from fallen branches, twigs and bits of cloth found when foraging

3. Ladder made from hemp rope or vines, steps from branches

Cave

4. Shall be near the coast or on a mountain
5. If near the coast should have enough land to store food

Washing, exercises, swimming, foraging, building shelter, learning about Mother earth and ocean, the Web of Life, writing letters, collecting items for wandering, learning how to build fires for cooking and warmth

Staff* (for walking), sack, sleeping roll, tin plate * tin cup* cooking pot (small), liquorice root, seed bag, herb bag, sewing kit (for mending), books on berries, mushrooms, herbs, survival, sewing kit, pictorial Feng Shui,* bamboo flute, black combat trousers, bee jumper (this was a favourite warm, blue & black striped jumper he had at the time), and spider hat (the items marked * are ones we purchased together for the move)

We began, by buying a map of the local area and one day I suggested we should go out for a walk in the woodlands and see if it was a place that might be suitable.

I could almost hear the psychiatrist saying the word 'colluding' again in my ear.

But I had a purpose to this plan, knowing how much Ben liked to feel safe and yet needed to know he still had some choices.

We went to a local wood between Cullompton and Exeter and began using the map to find the public rights of way. Some of the area was overgrown and quite steep and muddy in places. The weather that day was also not particularly warm. He enjoyed the closeness of the trees but after a while decided that he had done enough for that day.

We came home and I put the things we had begun to buy for his new venture into a box.

Because I had let him walk some way ahead of me just to feel he was not being 'kept on a lead' I think he began to realise just how isolated he would be if he chose this way of living.

I never got into a discussion about it and only answered his questions about the next trip out, with a calm plan of the day. When the weather was fine we would go out for short walks, as often as he felt comfortable.

Much later I would be able to take him regularly to Dartmoor or further, to Glastonbury Tor where he had once felt such a deep spiritual connection.

He never did go on his own to live in the woods but I think that he knew we would not prevent him from achieving what he felt able to accomplish.

All this would not have been possible, if we had agreed to having put him in a psychiatric hospital.

Whilst researching for this book I looked for evidence that being out in a green environment is more beneficial than being enclosed within the grey walls of a hospital setting, and I discovered the following taken from 'Psychology Today':

All that Glitters is not Gold How can urban environments without green space make us feel good?

Colin Ellard, Ph.D. October18th 2012

> 'The fact that exposure to green spaces is good for our brains and our bodies is hardly news these days. There is solid research showing that everything from a view of a potted plant to a walk through the woods can improve your mood, boost your thinking skills, and even lengthen your life. This research is critical because it provides us with reminders of the importance of finding the time to get outside and enjoy nature. In fact, at a meeting of the Healing Cities Institute that I attended a couple of years ago, one of the ideas on the table was that these kinds of experiences were so important that health care practitioners ought to be prescribing planned visits to natural spaces with the same care as (or perhaps as a substitute for) prescriptions for mood-altering drugs taken for depression or medications given to children to treat learning disabilities'.

He continues with his analysis that even cities can have their own dynamic atmosphere of social interaction and stimulating environments that can be beneficial.

As a contextual practising art graduate in the late 1990s, I would agree that a stimulating and buoyant environment within a city is of great value to the inhabitants, when there are no green spaces in which to relax. Yet the preference would always be to have as many trees around as possible, as it is a known fact that plane trees were planted in London to give shade and beauty to the streets, being more resistant to the polluted air of cities than other species because they shed their bark frequently.

Also the trees absorb CO_2, removing and storing the carbon, while releasing the oxygen back into the air. They also aid healing, as studies have shown that patients with views of trees out of their windows heal faster and with less complications. Children with ADHD show fewer symptoms when they have access to nature. Exposure to trees and nature aids concentration by reducing mental fatigue.

So my belief that to get out and enjoy the stimuli of nature and other inspiring places was certainly of great benefit.

Being able to visit a park or local open space where there are birds singing and a diversity of flowers and plants growing has a relaxing effect on everyone. We must fight to protect our ever diminishing parks where we live or the health of future generations will suffer, thus causing even more strain on the depleted health services.

However, Ben was needing more intellectual stimulation than I could supply, so I looked for other things that might encourage his more logical thinking processes.

It was the summer of 2000 and there was a Book Festival coming up at Dartington Hall. So I booked a slot to hear Alain Botton, the Philosopher, give a lecture on his recent book.

Although Ben found it difficult to concentrate, he did enjoy that day and later I managed to arrange some 'one to one' sessions with Alan Kirby, a writer in Totnes who had proposed a 'Walk & Talk' group. Although this group never materialised due to a lack of response to his advert, he met us after I wrote to him about Ben's mental state and so began a very positive and creative few months.

By the autumn we were regularly travelling to Totnes for sessions with Alan. Ben grew in confidence, through these private sessions and we, as a family, could see that this was an important part of the rediscovery of his abilities, a transformation from confusion to coherence. With great patience Alan would read through what Ben had written and they would discuss various points raised.

His style of writing was being taken seriously and he was learning once more to hold intellectual critiques.

Ben felt valued again. We owe a debt of gratitude to Alan for his kind assistance in helping Ben to write in a more structured way and to take time to discuss various viewpoints that arose.

Andrew Barkla at the Exeter branch of the 'Hearing Voices Network' as it was known, would also make Ben feel welcome. They called their own group the 'Joan of Arc Room' and were proud of the famous French voice-hearer. From the moment we first met them we realised here was a group of people who would not only understand how Ben was suffering but might help in someway to alleviate the accompanying fears that dogged him.

It was arranged that each week Ben would attend their meetings and he gradually came to enjoy the opportunities that this group provided. The welcoming atmosphere of inclusion and acceptance is still a very encouraging part of the atmosphere of what is now the Bridge Collective.

It includes a wider range of mental perceptions in the sessions and has many other creative groups within its framework, such as Andrew's 'Greenwood Project' where people can enjoy the quiet of being outdoors while making things from natural elements found in the woods. Many a tasty meal is cooked over an open fire.

There is also a Women's Art Group 'Open Minds' which is a forum-based group where discussions between the members can take place; 'Rainbow Bridge' which respects diversity of gender, 'Underground Sounds' for musical experience and enjoyment, 'Open Afternoon' where just dropping in for a chat is welcomed and 'Community Meeting' where views can be aired in a safe and accepting environment.

Ben was instrumental in founding the music group known as the 'Underground Sounds' where people can share ideas and enjoy making or listening to music in a relaxed and friendly setting.

So he began to find out more about what the HVN could offer and, in November 2000, we both attended a seminar in Gloucester to hear Ron Coleman speak about his own prescribed illness and road to recovery.

Ron Coleman states in his books and on the internet that voice hearing is not strange or a reason to diagnose 'madness' but should be viewed as a different perception than what is considered the 'norm'. That this ability could if given the correct management actually enhance the life of the voice-hearer. Even when voices are troubling they can with training become more manageable and so not dominate the life of the voice-hearer so as to interrupt daily life. He goes on to explain how the mindset of the NHS system as we know it actually increases the idea of being 'sick' and through its treatment encourages a reliance on being given labels for mental health. During his many hospital incarcerations he became a 'good schizophrenic'. In other words the system treating him conditioned him to *be* that person; to *wear* that label.

He also states that the person for whom the diagnosis of mad has been attributed must learn to *own* their experience and take control of what they are able to cope with at each step, so that eventually they can stop being the ill person with no power and be the person who takes ownership of who they are and decide how to move forward, finding ways to *work* with their fears and perceptions.

Ron is now Director of 'Working to Recovery' and with Karen Taylor and others they have been instrumental in setting up training events world-wide offering many solutions for recovery to all parts of the community where they are needed.

Meeting Ron Coleman had a significant effect on Ben's own understanding of his voice hearing and offered hope. He could see that it was possible to rise above the prognosis of the professionals and take back control for himself. Not succumbing to the doctors pressure of an ever more strongly medicated and controlled life. Ben now wanted to explore ways of understanding how to cope with and even use these voices as part of his recovery experience.

At the Conference we attended, I purchased a workbook devised by Ron Coleman as an aid to recovery. Ben never did use it but the principles of what it contained were, in some ways, already being put into practice during Ben's time with Alan Kirby.

Dr. Tim Harlow, our family GP, had written many letters over the years supporting Ben and ourselves as his carers and was, once again, extremely helpful when we were desperate for Ben to receive some kind of 'talking' therapy other than that which we had engaged in so far. He understood the beneficial value of the Psychologist assigned so briefly to Ben and in a letter to me, dated February 2001, we were sent details of Richard Skinner.

Richard was to enable Ben to relax and talk freely and without fear of further medication. These sessions would prove an absolute godsend, as the waiting list Ben was on for Cognitive Behavioural Therapy seemed to be extending rather than diminishing with the years.

I remember sitting in the car while Ben visited Richard and feeling so grateful to know that Ben would progress and gain confidence with this talking therapy. I never asked what had transpired in those meetings but could tell as he came out looking less troubled that it was working.

Richard Skinner now describes himself on his website as a researcher, poet and performer, having retired from mental health work and also part-time work in a bookshop. Richard certainly helped Ben to gather his thoughts together, giving him the tools and ability to manage his future.

The journeys Ben and I took and pleasant lunches enjoyed in quiet surroundings away from the many stresses suffered, all played a part in bring our son back to 'life'. Walking and Talking is still one of the finest examples of free health choices we can make.

7

Ben's Own Words and Pictures up to 2004

In this chapter you will find several different kinds of ways that Ben has expressed his thoughts. All have been included with his permission. Each sample is used to illustrate, that despite being considered 'mentally ill' during much of the time, he was very creative. His work is both erudite and sometimes even amusingly observant about his situation.

The first piece was written when he was living away from home whilst studying at South Downs College in Waterlooville. He explained to me that for some years before his official 'University Breakdown' he felt he had been going 'strange'.

On the next page is one of Ben's strange letters, written in his own form of language. He had always been fascinated by language and was often frustrated that there were not the right words to explain what he wanted to say. He liked to experiment with the many ways words could be written, especially if they had two or even three meanings.

Then there is a solitary diary entry and a short story written in 1998 and before his serious psychosis. This is followed by poems, essays and a short 'sketch' of his 'voices'. Various pencil/crayon drawings which he produced when he was living at home in Devon whilst waiting for therapy, appear throughout. The last two pictures are of the trees he painted when in Primary School.

The chapter ends with a letter he wrote thanking his professor of studies for his help and support. Ben had made one final attempt to gain a degree in psychology and social studies, this time at Exeter University, having obtained good grades in the pre degree

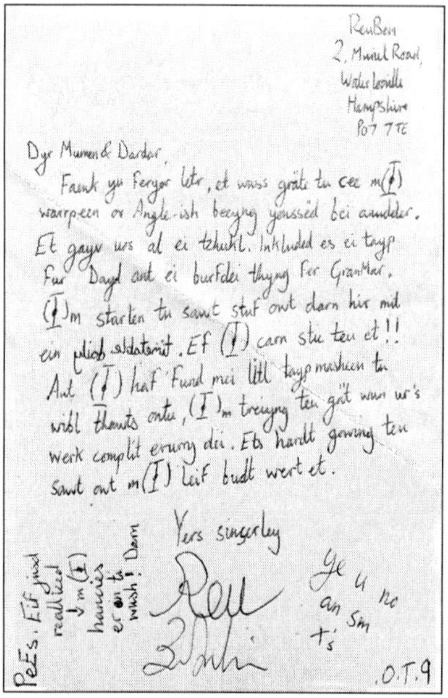

RenBen
2, Muriel Road,
Waterlooville
Hampshire
Po7 7TE

Dyr Mumm& Dardar,

Faank yu fer yor letr, et wass grate tu cee m(I) warrpeen ov Angle-ish beeyng youssed bei awdder. Et gayv urs al ei tchukl. Inkluded es ei tayp fur Dayd ant ei burfdei thyng fer GranMar. (I)m starten tu sawt stuf owt darn hir mid ein pliod oldatemit. Ef (I) cam stu teu et!! Ant (I) haf fund mei littl taypmasheen tu wibl thawts ontu, (I)m treiyng ten git wun ur's werk complit evreny dei. Ets hardt gowing ten sawt owt m(I) leif budt wert et.

Yers singerley

Ren

Ye 4 ne an Sm +s

PeEs. Eif just reallized (I) m(I) hanies er on to wash! Dam

.O.T.9

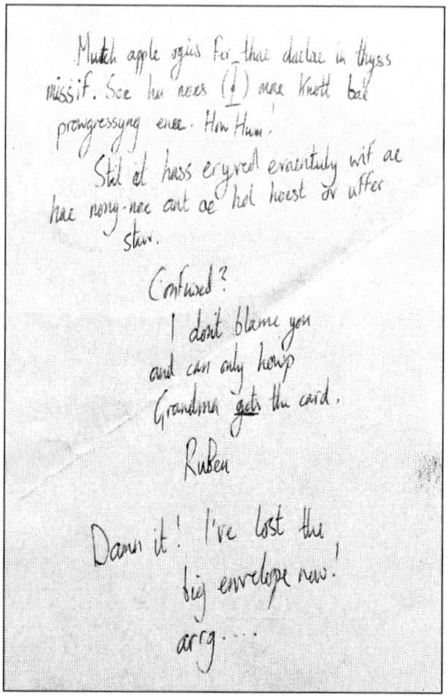

Mutch apple ogies fer that daelae in thyss missif. See hu nees (I) mae knott bee prowgressyng enee. Hm Hum!

Stil et hass ergyrell evantuly wif ae hae nowy-nee ant ae hel hoest or uffer stuv.

Confused?

I dont blame you and can only howp Grandma gets the card.

Ruben

Damn it! I've lost the big envelope now! arrg....

course he attended. Once more he was thwarted by the problems arising from 'too much time being spent in his head' during the necessary studies for this. So he had to leave and find another way to pursue his goal to seek answers and lead others to a more fulfilling future.

Ben's Diary Entry from 22nd February 1998

I hope this diary may have some effect upon those who read it as it contains all my most pressing thoughts and theories unencumbered by any need to appear perfect in my own eyes. It is by these eyes that I have sought for some explanation of my present existence.

I have not two eyes only, whose very nature limits perception to a small range of frequencies. I have a third eye, as do all humankind, which physically brings great awareness of light.

I feel as if emerging from some terrible depression that I have become acquainted with during the darkening months. These represent to me a time of dying as each year a radical shift in personality is affected much like reincarnation. My third eye sees this process directly and brings it to my attention. New energy fills my soul in the coming of the waking year.

Banner produced by some members of the group
during a day event at the Joan of Arc Room

Two examples of Ben's artwork

Above: Kneeling Man. Below: Landscape 2

Landscape 1

Portrait

Untitled

Childhood painting. Tree 1

Childhood painting. Tree 2

Every year I die in winter to be reborn in spring. It is now approaching evening and as per usual I can focus more on my existence as I feel it dying for another day. Despite the regularity of such ?

I don't get bored, nor am I aware of them at every moment.

Every moment has its own death and I can scarcely be aware of its passing, except in the sensation of vague dissatisfaction with the use I have put to each. Day after day I will bemoan the ineffectual results. The year fades with fascination , with incomplete anticipations.

When actually involved with the process of existence it is not in my nature to reflect so.

Today I was far too involved with the nag of tobacco-withdrawal to consider the identity of that sensation.

When possessed by one of those alien presences it can be hard to focus and consequently it is left till this evening of reflection to perceive with a bit more clarity the time being I am not in the grip once more.

Perhaps it is the rhythm of this personality that niggles so, but it to passes into winter and ceases (for a time).

Such possessions do not always arise from an external source, my sense of self too, possesses this physical body by a number of means.

The imitation of self upon the rigours of motion result in shatters of me crystallised to form a mirror.

Without this body my self would remain unfulfilled, this pen not held. Without this self my body would cease to move with any cohesion. This symbiotic relationship has resulted in a pearl of identity. The random chance of events physical and temporal connected in a hideous dance with tranquil and still awareness. Is this my true centre?

Ah if only it were that simple. I am may be still but it moves through time which is not > I am relative to I am < Another mirror, grains of crystal rub together and there is even more irritation.

Sometimes of course this can be pleasant.

Until tomorrow then. . .

He wrote no more entries in this diary but did write the following short and quite telling story. . .

Looking into the mirror, the dishevelled man yawned and scratched his forehead until flakes marred the not unattractive features. The sun streamed through the window warming his face slightly, behind him a small ginger cat yawned contently and looked at the slouching figure.

The man was often called Taemer, by those few acquaintances he had seen fit to get close enough, to what most would consider transient friendship. It was not in his nature to mourn his inadequacies, he had known nought else and he could have looked upon the derogatory statements of those who did, with some confusion.

At least his cat Salmon was wise enough never to comment on his malformed character, except to complain when sat upon (which happened all too frequently)

Taemer struggled to marshal his insufficient will power enough, to approach the washing bowl and douse his face with the tepid water.

The cat grew bored of the ritualistic toilet and padded away towards the door, looking back with some affection upon a grumbling frame silhouetted in the light of dawn.

Salmon didn't much care for the wintry gust of wind coming from the window in the hallway, she pounced onto the sill anyway with the barest mew of contempt at the aesthetic failings of the season.

Already there was movement in the streets below, at odds with the languid pace of her own and the downright laziness of Taemer's preferred way of life.

She noted the harsh outline of one of these figures and the angry swirl that followed in its wake. This was not unusual in the inhabitants of this place, but the eyes glowed with a ferocity she had come to recognise in the most tragic of such self important humans. At once arrogant and distant to those who were unfortunate enough to be in his surroundings. This man would demand recognition without recognising.

He wore a green tunic cut close to the skin with slightly flared sleeves and loose trousers with distinct creases, indicating in subtle ways, an obsessive character.

The face was angular and stern with a sharp nose that protruded in a singularly unbecoming fashion, hair tied back to accentuate this most unappealing of features.

This fearful apparition was approaching Taemer's lodgings with some determination, which meant at best, confrontation.

This was not good, he was forever testing Taemer's patience which although abundant, was not inexhaustible.

Salmon knew that today was not going to be a relaxing one and looking down the hallway she could see that her companion was barely dressed and not at all prepared for the angular man's rather disruptive nature.

As the heavy steps punished the wood of the stairway, she made a dash for the security afforded by the space under the bed.

I am not too sure when Ben wrote 'Homework', but it seems yet another exploration into double meanings and word manipulation. Apparently he remembers being quite ill at the time. The title is just a reference to schooldays, but he told me it was *not* written while at school.

Homework

Most people think I'm just like them, but x=x+1. I am reborn with every morning, an addition of myself, a tumescent pubescent? No guides to tell me where I'm going, but I have friends who wear signposts around their heads. This way, and I'll go to sleep upon a stream of consciousness; that way, and I'll scream with sensation; another way and I'll see through the lies. Freedom rests upon a path I'm not taught, the path of becoming.

If I gaze into the blackboard long enough will it gaze back into me? A curious way of acquiring knowledge I know, but I'd rather remember the truth inside than force the outside in. Maybe the teacher saw me, but he's still learning and won't see below the tip of my pointy head. I'm a dunce in the corner, backed into a corner and some wonder why I snarl.

Let me see, let me hear, let me sense and feel. When will the profession end and the confession begin? Mr. Savage, let's begin with you. A spinal injury that's made you a laughing stock to yourself, physical education become interior design<>ate a successor to stay on top a little bit longer? At least he's honest, unlike Miss Fox who's just too chicken to face her true nature.

Tell me about God as if you know; I like the sound of a blown trumpet in the mouth of a grown strumpet. He wears a collar, but he's wearing knickers. He's wet them more than me, because he knows he knows nothing, but doesn't want to admit it. Teachers teaching nothing? How preposterous, but that's my lesson as I fail the test of faith, I might just scrape a 'be'.

In-Glish teaches us rules, R absolute, R relative, R pointless, but I don't blame them. It's the guv'nor's mental standards that make us straight as a die and so we do, creatively. I'm not a man, so I must be a mouse in Lenny's hand. He's fond but he fondled my brain with those big fat fingers (not exactly surgery) and George has to mark my work. Expand my horizons beyond the lore as I get thrown away.

Mary Mary quite contrary, wise to the norm, but not a part torn apart by the con sensual touch. Look outside the gates and see the Garden glow beneath a son of science, genetic manipulation conkers? Internal infernal still at large. Eye won't conform to what eye see, but sum do p=? All ways question, but an answer just breeds more questions. It's not the quantity, but the quality that earns a qualification. . .

Whilst going through a whole case of now indecipherable notebooks, many with Ben's previously scrawled writing I came across a short 'sketch' he had written on the computer. I have no date, but was probably produced during the time he was struggling with his identity during his first semester at University. Having previously talked to him about my own search for my birth family, I had let slip that when he was born we had discussed naming him Rueben. How we later thought he might find this name mocked when he went to school. So we named him Benjamin instead. I think this may have had more of an effect on him than I realised at the time. Anyway the following sketch he wrote is an illustration of how a creative mind can work through all the voices in his head, as they are just parts of himself.

Tally's Book

<u>Dramatis Personae</u>

Tally a poet
Ming a manimal
ReuBen an unborn
Benjamin a madman
Marigold a flower

<u>The Conversation</u>

Marigold: Ben, can you hear me?
Benjamin: What? Who's that?
Marigold: Down here, I need to talk to you.
Benjamin: Oh, hello! What can I do for you?

Marigold: I'm not long for this world and I wondered if you could help me with a few questions that need to be cleared up.
Benjamin: But of course! I shall do my best to be of some use to you, so what is it you want to know?
Marigold: I want to know what happens when I die, I want to know what God is, I want to know why I'm here. All the classic problems that have to be faced before one can leave the world a wise soul.
Benjamin: That will be a hard task for me as I am not sure I'm up to the job. It wasn't wisdom that led me to madness, that I am sure about. Why ask a fool such difficult questions? Questions he himself cannot satisfy with answers?
Marigold: I think you know more than you profess to know. I know you think deeply about these matters and I know that great wisdom comes from madness, so please, indulge me with your foolishness.
Benjamin: Very well, I shall do my best and hope that is enough to see me through. I shall relate to you a conversation I once overheard whilst listening to my head and that it will allay your fears and solve those problems you have.
ReuBen: I'm glad you two are here. I've been told that soon it shall be time for me to incarnate in a form of my own. I shall no longer be a dream in a madman's mind. Can you tell me what it's going to be like as I'm already forgetting what this man knows and I'm becoming scared of what is to come.
Tally: Most assuredly we can talk, it's not often one of us gets that kind of opportunity and it is always those closest who are called on to advise.
Ming: And we have known you for just over two years and shared many good times.
Tally: Tell us, what is it you would like to know?
ReuBen: There are so many things I need to discuss. Can I just bombard you with questions?
Ming: Certainly, we don't mind.
ReuBen: OK then, what is the meaning of a day?
Tally: A day is a lifetime in miniature. When you wake in the morning you are confused and don't know which world you're supposed to be in. Being born is much like that. By noon when the sun is shining at it's fullest, the splendour of youthful vigour is achieved and as the afternoon progresses more is accomplished. By the evening it has come time to reminisce and relax into the dim

glow of old age and then at night it has come time to go into a different world with different rules. This is life, a series of days and this is existence a series of incarnations. By the end of seventy or more years, none has the excuse of fear for daily there is a lifetime to live.

ReuBen: Are there any more examples demonstrating reincarnation in the life of a mortal?

Ming: Yes there are, for example if you have read much Dickens you will hear that man refer to life as a river flowing out to sea, the communion of all the waters of the world.

ReuBen: How then is this an example of reincarnation? It doesn't sound like one to me.

Ming: Because the cycle does not end in the sea. Clouds form out there and return the water to the land.

Tally: And this reminds one of Empedocles' teaching that we are formed from a mixing and intermixing of different elements. Different waters mix in the sea and return to land in different configurations and so reminds us that we are never the same again.

ReuBen: Never the same again?

Tally: The component parts will all be you, but not always the same you as existed before. Each aspect will have existed in many forms, some will have existed for longer, some will be more primitive, others more refined. Each will bond together to create a person who will in turn express a higher principle because it will be an aspect of greater unity, greater community.

Ming: I do believe we're getting a bit beyond ourselves. Should we not consider other proofs for reincarnation?

Tally: I hear the word proofs, does this mean we're to discuss a scientific perspective also?

ReuBen: It looks like we might have to. After all I am to be incarnated into a society which venerates the scientific principle.

Tally: Well then, let's take a principle which science holds to be eternal. To my mind this can only be energy. It is never created, never destroyed, it transforms from one state to another and can be transmitted from one body to another.

ReuBen: How then does this relate to reincarnation?

Tally: It means that you are eternal, you change state from a potential being to a kinetic one. This process is eternal itself, shifting from a state of potential to kinetic. It extends from the relatively swift interchanges of physical and spiritual life to the rebirth of cosmic principles.

Ming: Don't forget how this principle is enacted in the physical world. How consumption is rebirth...
Tally: You had better explain that. You are after all an expert in the field of consumption.
Ming: Each being is filled with energy which you might call the eternal soul of a creature. Whenever you consume a living being or one who was until recently alive, you are consuming their essential soul energy. This makes you stronger for they nourish your system with their entire being. All the energy you express is the result of consumption in some way. Naturally then the nature of the soul in question is important. Your soul, their soul, what exactly are you? Are you what you eat?
ReuBen: That's a rather worrying thought, I don't want to be eaten!
Ming: But think what an ennobled worm it is that eats of your decomposing flesh. That worm becomes filled with human energy. How fine a fate for such a lowly creature!
Tally: You don't make it clear which creature you think lowly, the human or the worm. Anyway Ming, calm down you're practically foaming at the mouth. Let us discuss instead the role of genetic rebirth.
ReuBen: That's a good subject to study as I am a bit worried about some aspects of my DNA that's forming in the dream below...
Tally: Your genetic line is reproduced in you via the DNA of your parents. Each parent's DNA contains memories of the basic building blocks of each of your ancestors and each of these ancestors has a primal voicing which has an effect upon the soul in question. Some can be particularly strong, usually those of the most recent memory-selves, but also more ancient memories can have very strong personalities and can play a role in the developing line over successive generations. Some can even be strong enough to reincarnate themselves into the captain's seat, because of a memory occupying an important area in the DNA. It may remain latent for many generations and then reawaken at any time.
ReuBen: Does a soul have any control of the matter or is the decision made for him?
Tally: The soul can align itself with a particular gene-memory if it so wishes, yet much is out of our control in the matter.
Ming: I remember when this boy we inhabit, slept with the bedclothes over his head and kept his glasses on as a child, only to discover that his father did the same thing when he was a child. Ben did this without knowing, so where did this ritual develop?

Tally: Good point Ming. I think you've earned a little more time on your favourite subject, but please make it relevant.
Ming: Sometimes you can be insufferable! But at least now I get the chance to put a few words in and take some away from you!
ReuBen: Calm down lads, you're here to enlighten me, you're not here to fight. I don't have much time, so no more distractions!
Ming: Sorry, I do apologise ReuBen. OK, how does consumption relate to DNA? It's not an important factor, yet still significant that the energy used to create the sperm and egg must be generated from energy acquired in the eating process. This energy leaves a faint signature to the successful sperm and the egg it impregnates. These memories may be insignificant on their own, but when they are collected at the end of the food chain they can become more potent. Animal memories, vegetable memories, mineral memories. My boy, you're going to become a living memory!
ReuBen: Surely we should also talk about that force that unites into a coherent self, rather than a babbling barrage of memory-noise in the head. What is it? Tell me before I start thinking I don't exist.

Tantalisingly, the story ends, just as one hopes for an answer. But that perhaps, was intended.

The following notes and essay were written while Ben was at University. He believes it was never marked, as it did not fit the criteria of an analysis of Plato's Philosophy. He had become increasingly detached from reality.

Paradox

Para Dox waging war behind enemy lines. Hunting in the forest Para chases his Ideals, rejecting distractions until he dies. In another part of the forest he awakes to begin the chase again, dying and waking until eventually he does. When rested they awaken, their Ideals once again the quarry. Dox sits and waits for her Ideals, rejecting the distortions until one sits with her and they wait for the next.

This Pair o'ducks flew overhead, but this world wanted only one, shooting at them until. . . Para Dox came down to land.

Will they classify me and pin me to a tree as a classy<>fiction?

Plato & Epistemology Essay 1

There are flickering shadows upon the walls of our caves. Plato's dream imagery has manifestations in the physical or what some would call the 'real' world. It is a matter of perception to shift the dreams of existence into that physical reality, or as Lewis Carroll indicated, of going through the looking glass. With the aid of these powerful dream images my perspective can be shifted in relationship to the physical world and this is how it came about.

Medusa and the Bees

I was seated in Aneesh's Playpen, one cave amongst many that has been imprinted with its particular dream-reality. To see this 'reality' is a matter of acceptance that it is there. The television was on and my attention shifted between that and the lit candles in the fireplace. Of that I shall elucidate further at a later stage of this journey into my tail.

The candles appeared so much more real than the shifting lights emitted by the flickering screen and it was the moment that Plato's dream became a physical reality for me. The television set occupied the modern day equivalent of the flickering shadows in Plato's allegory of the Cave, stating and re-stating 'truths' from one particular perception of reality. The irony of the situation was that Aneesh had often quoted Plato as her favourite philosopher, and yet here she was sitting in her cave watching the shadow play. At present she is unwilling to leave her cave, for she appears to have been chained within it. This is a 'real' situation and yet exists on the other side of my looking glass, the imagery of dreams.

At the moment of realisation, flickering shadows became uncomfortable to gaze upon. As I looked about I noticed that all had been turned to stone.

Once again the dream shifted and the television was now Medusa. The shadows were her hissing snakes and behind my looking glass I was not turned , as others had been. She could not see me hidden behind my own mirror, for she is but a reflection herself. If I should sneak quietly, would it be possible to behead that fascinating muse that can turn another's dreams to stone? Oh what japes! But that would mean to become a hunter in the kingdom of Human-Animals. So her time will come later when my own cave, filled with fears is left behind.

My dream shifted again then and the flickering became a dancing of bees, communicating with the hive-mind dreams of sweet nectar. These caves became cells of drones, serving Queen Bee to secure her fertility. Medusa was ever jealous of others fertile dreams and having evaded her watery grave now ruled the airwaves, usurping the throne of the true Hive-Queen. And so with stolen vitality she infected our cells and made our dreams infertile, unrealised.

Let us now return to the fireplace, for it was by this means that this particular journey through the looking-glass began. It's dimensions reveal much. The candles had been placed in the gateway where fires had been built in the past. Today, only candles, tomorrow any other object of attention. One image to be the focus of the journey. Yet again it merely takes awareness of other gateways to make the dream a reality for yourself: but it was always there.

Around the gateway were carved images, these served to act as a guide for perceiving the nature of the fireplaces gateway. This is not necessarily required if a different path suggests itself. It was on a different, earlier occasion that I noticed the carvings. In the centre, the shape of an eye, perception was offered to those who might notice. On either side a being seated in a vehicle, the vehicle of the minds eye. One appeared to face outwards and the other faced away from me, an inner reality of dreams presented in the forms of the physical world. These two reflections from the eye, revealed that the looking-glass shows both sides in much the same way that the physical eye is a perceptual form that translates through mirror-images as any optician or biologist will tell you. These two reflections of the same entity existed in a watery world bordered by shorelines, displayed in the carving of wave-like forms and boundaries. Our minds flow the physical and the inner world of dreams, yet they both exist in the sea of consciousness.

Below the watery world was carved the physical, immediately below the split entity on both sides was a head of bestial features, our connection to the hunting-grounds of survival. Below that a tree carved by cunning craft into a club, a compromise between ideal dream and physical limitations. Finally an acorn, the seed of wisdom that exists in the kingdom of matter. These lower levels had only one facing, for they lacked a direct connection to the perceptual world. The seed of wisdom could only take its true form in the mind's eye, the perceiver of light that does not overlook the truth in the physical, but rather extends that truth as a reality to the beholder.

What then is this light the mind's eye doth perceive? Is it this which is the gateway to the world of ideal forms that Plato envisioned whilst dancing in the sun? And how does it reveal its existence but through the form of dreams, an internal light in the darkness of sleep. Both images in the looking-glass require light. The physical has the glowing orbs of fireflies if daylight is scarce. The dream has perceptual lights from the mind's eye. Look in the mirror, what do you see?

Some are strangers to their dreams, looking-glasses distorted and cracked under Medusa's gaze. With infertile dreams they seek to emulate this usurper and serve her as drones, the beautiful dead. Oh, how Medusa does cherish her prizes for her cave then dances with shadows. Her shard of reflected light hides from its own reflection and masquerade as the light itself: and yet she lacks connection to the looking-glass gateway outside of her cave in the sunlight. Does she hide because she is jealous of dreams that are not hers? She holds but her own in vain pride, afraid to become the gateway, afraid of losing herself through the looking-glass. She is trapped in the physical world or "reality" as some may call it and like Aesop's fable of the Fox who lost his tail, similarly seeks to convince others that it's a good idea. And so some hate their reflections for they have become chained to Medusa's infertile dream. And what do I see?

Gardening For Idiots

Upon a hill it came to pass that a speck of glass grew into a tree.

The tree coiled and spread wings of reflection. The wings were mirrors fragmentary. Branches of shard like leaves were strong and beautiful. One day there came Monkey wandering in the forest about the hill. He looked up and saw this striking and individual tree, deciding there and then to make it his home.

Time passed and Monkey sat on a branch, admiring his surroundings. The fruit of summer fell to the ground, resolving a part of a part of a cycle. Monkey caught one of the glittering leaves and admired his reflection. It cut into his hands however and blood poured from his wounds. Unconcerned was Monkey, for fascination can be strong indeed; two red rivers flowed and fed the tree. Monkey slept with closed (I).

Cuckoo flew in the skies above the forest and was, like Monkey drawn to this singular tree. Seeing its simian fellow she grew envious and not appreciating its own beauty, Cuckoo brought forth a jealous seed and planted it within Monkey, becoming a new heartbeat. The rivers became a flood and Monkey awoke startled, crying out in sorrow.

Now all he had was pain and Cuckoo had the reflection.

Gradually Monkey's wailing became the cackle of Cuckoo, his body sickened whilst all around life blossomed. Jester saw this peculiar sight as he came dancing along the earthen path. He began to laugh at this sorry creature gazing with rheumy eyes at the fruit of a year long dead, oblivious to the once again blossoming tree.

The laughter infuriated Cuckoo with such an easy and open character for her own charms became unpleasant in its presence. Cuckoo's retorts however only served to make Jester laugh yet louder as he danced around the hill ever upwards, Cuckoo was overwhelmed and shrunk from view.

Monkey felt empty, having no more volition, vocation or values than a corpse. Jester chuckled with good-humoured charity and offered the flower that grew from its spine. As Monkey took hold of this bloom, the cutting shard of glass fell from his grasp and the flower filled his wounds. Within him it's roots formed a new tree banishing Cuckoo and sending it to flight (for now). Monkey fell inside the tree and now became a speck, then a chuckle and dancing to become Jester.

The Sun And The Sea

Gazing at the firefly on the wall in this hive constructed of wax in this our Ether Lamp, I see a moth. His goal is oblivion through a flaming gateway, the dream of moths. And what is a philosopher's dream? This dream I recount is a flapping wing, for a moth I be. Dancing in the sunlight, I know nothing and yet everything to learn in the gateways of the looking-glass. I do not see Medusa and she not me. I am free to dance, my dreams unturned. But what is cast in the flapping of my wings? Shadows to those below, other dancers create more. Each moth seeks nothing, a non-sense, but to those below I can only say 'Don't search for it in our shadows and proclaim that we made sense.'

And so saying, my attention shifts to this page. As I make shapes in the sand fresh from swimming in the sea, dreams and the bed become impermanent both. The gateway exists in all things if you can so see it, yet I cannot hold the water for it slips through my fingers and I accept that it is so. The sand slips through my fingers too, so why hold onto that? I can reach no conclusions, for sandcastles they be and return to the sea. Scratched words in the sand or a wave from the sea, which to be, they're both me.

Plato was afeared of changes wrought by the sea, for he thought that the end of his sandcastle was the end of an ideal form. Yet is it possible to ward off change with sandbanks of legislation? His dream is a Playdoh Republic, the ideals exist yet their forms are changed. Dreams mould the Republic and they can never manifest in their entirety for we are both sides of the looking-glass. Are we the little hands that emerge from waves to shift the sand? Dreams re-arrange old forms for none of our creations manifest the sea of consciousness in one wave, for the sea is all of them in concert. Our wave plays games in the sand for we do not fear and why do we not fear?

Aquarium Dreams

Are you sitting comfortably? Then I'll begin. . . The Sun in the Sea is but a bubble and yet also glistens with brightness on the surface and eerie in depth. Strange flows in the hidden wave where language is new.

Below the surface in a small, dark cave Playdoh Republic gloried in it's air-trap. It was hidden so from the glistening that it created its own lights, fireflies indeed Playdoh, brittle under the assault of the flies was a constraining fight for the line. There was not enough room and ugly it became.

The Sun in the Sea braved many dangers, yet he laughed at the world in his cheery way. Laughter for he was a jester of the ocean, a Sea lion in the eerie glow of the fireflies. Sea lion reached the shoreline and played games in the sand, yet an altogether different game presented itself with this Republic.

Playdoh had for many years been re-shaped within its original guidelines and had become a crazed construction of tunnels. Sea lion could not fit himself into any of the specifically shaped holes and became trapped. They were not too keen in the Republic of course, but sandcastles left too long become unpleasant anyway. Another inhabitant of the cave, King Newt was smitten with this strange home that he had guarded for the flies, for he appreciated their aesthetic. And so he snarled at the playful, childish newcomer. Of course King Newt was terrified, for no waves had emerged since he had been washed up long ago on a wave from the rivers that once had flowed. This is when it would happen then, for he had sickened from an encroachment of this unpleasant brine. It had been but a trickle once, but now it had become a flood. Lands had sunk beneath the sea before and now the waters had become very deep. What had once been a garden for foolish apes was now a cave for crafty flies.

This decrepit creature fought hard, or so he thought. Sea lion however hardly noticed for the flies did burn his eyes with their hatred of strangers. They burnt him as they burnt their Republic. Sickened their protector as they had their home with unpleasing odours and ghastly residue. Seal ion was a sensitive soul, more used to the rhythm of the waves, but he was trapped now in an alien environment Flexing his tail wildly in panic he cried in pain. The call was made, Mother Ocean heard her child. Many more had been similarly inconvenienced on the island and in the caves of decaying lands.

Thunderous tidal flows came in response and King Newt's guardianship was at an end. He was taken by the flow to the MemorSee, to learn how to swim in this his new home. His sandcastle was gone to become the seabed. His beloved fireflies transformed into explorers, travellers in the wave. The Flies had become star-plankton and their Playdoh Republic? Well, some new child would one day come and play on the beach again. But what you say happened to Sea lion? Mother Ocean's children played tricks on each other and couldn't care less about sandcastles, for they never turned out right.

P.S. Before you mark this ask >no< lest you say >know<.

Linguistic Key:

<> Read word separately or together >< Read backwoods or four woods

(I) Personal I, Communal I, Universal I and uncertainty of distinctions between them

The following poems are selected from Ben's writings, again illustrating how he uses words like an artist would colours, mixing and changing their meanings according to his thoughts.

FOR MARIA

Our Paths have cross'd
and nothing's lost
For <-> eve<-> return <-> all
to the flow
erring fools that we are
twining Ka
more to show time to go
all to be, river meets THE sea
lion, the beach, in the son

Farewell

§

I just want to be happy
And make you happy too,
I'm tired of all the pain.
It's in me always,
But so's the love,
The dream of an ideal form.
Of expression held in,
The blankness that kills
Like a field between us.
It happened, misfortune,
So many times I cried
And died inside a little bit.
Each time I froze,
Behaviour erratic,
Trying to cope.
Hope this time is different,
My being expressed so open.
The door way outside the norm,
All it takes
To be grabbed, nuzzled and warmed
By the fire of your contact
From another world.
Dream, drink the nectar
And drowse in the evening sun,
Of time in comfort and company,
Each a song in the symphony.

Underground

I. Down the mouse hole
watch the moles,
How they dig, dig
the sound underground
II. Mr. Rabbit said He had a head
He had a Head
It wasn't dead.
III. It called the dreams
down
From Heaven's Crown.
IV. To this bed-seed
To this bed-seed
Cure Man's greed
With a clown
a cloud
Speaks a loud
its sound
UndergRound.
V. Watch the roots gRowN
and the sea<>son sown
with the rain the sane
shown
the eRa of their ways,
And what must go.

§

The following is a short piece written by Ben for the 'All Write' section of the *Stepping Stones News*, a paper for those attending the NSF run day service called 'The Old Bakery' in Tiverton. The date is March 2000.

Confessions of a Manimal

I suppose it began with a meditation and my continual search for some clue to the puzzle of existence. For a number of years I had been massaging my third eye, relaxing and entering waking dreams, as I sought visions and past lives.

This time was different, closer, an experience I was only to understand much later.

I sat meditating in my chair when I heard a voice offering to let me join the human animals, an offer that I was not entirely unattracted to. Unfortunately, as I drifted to the source of this voice, I sensed a disconnection from all around me and a yawning black pit. Desperately I fought back to the surface and reminded myself of the world of physical reality, yet something remained of the horror, but another presence was there, a presence that said it would take away the malevolence and over the next few days I returned to normal.

As I sought sleep one morning following my night shift, I entered a meditative trance as I had done so many times in the past. This time I continued my relaxation for longer than I had done before and I felt my hands cross over my stomach though I knew they had not moved from beside my body. My mind started playing tricks on me in other ways. I found myself in the sky of another world and being approached by what I can only describe as an angel. It was an awe inspiring sight and the being though small, was massive in proportion. In my fear I asked it for a name and it uttered 'Transformation'. I asked its purpose, it uttered again,'Transformation'. I asked it many questions and to each it replied the same way. Once my questions had been exhausted I felt I was waiting for something and so I said 'Ok, transform me then,' in a rather testy manner. It was then that a fire flowed through the whole of my body and I awoke.

Notes dictated from Ben's comments regarding the effects of his prescribed medications - January 2003

One of the functions of my current medication (amisulpiride) is to control and suppress Dopamine levels in the brain. This has the effect of inhibiting passion and will power. They have this effect on humans and animals regardless of diagnosis or mental condition. Ref/pages 136-137 Toxic Psychiatry by Dr. Peter Breggin.

It is well known that long term use of such drugs exposes the patient to a high risk of tardive dyskinesia, tardive dementia and other permanent disabilities. I feel that not enough is being done to monitor the effects of drugs on my physical as well as psychiatric condition, either now or towards my long term care.

What neuroleptics do not do is control the effect of DMT [Dimethyltryptamine] secretions of the pineal gland. For instance it is known that familiar effects of recreational DMT creates a fifteen minute 'trip' into 'Hyperspace' where people report meeting the 'Self-Transforming Machine Elves.'

Evidence for this in my case, is a subjective one of voices telling me that I was never given permission to open the 'third eye', otherwise known as the pineal gland. That it was only supposed to open during sleep and that it would take them a long time to close it.

My very real and non-recreational experience has lasted much longer. I would therefore like to see more research into the chemical effects of existing neuroleptic medication, that so far only focuses on the dopamine levels of the brain, whilst allowing large amounts of DMT to affect the waking hours of patients with this distressing complaint.

What is needed, is to bring a balance back of DMT to the sleep pattern.

In 2001 I attended a conference in Winchester on Psychosis and Spirituality. A para psychologist explained her research into the pineal gland, saying that it only normally opened at night and also the chemical activity and is the creation of DMT which is known to be hallucinogenic, related to LSD, but thirty times stronger.

Abnormal pineal gland secretions release pinoline which then bonds with broken down serotonin in its form of DMT, which is normally only present during dream states. However in my case, it occurs during waking hours which gives rise to hallucinations.

Later, reading in the *Encyclopaedia Britannica* under the heading 'DMT' I noticed that DMT is sometimes found in the bodies of Schizophrenics. This has led me to believe that there is a strong justification in pursuing the study of this pineal gland in conjunction with dopamine activity in the brain and the effects of chemical change from the use of medication.

I would like the medical experts in neurology to seriously explore this theory.

I still hear voices. None of the medications prescribed to people like myself seems to prevent this phenomena. This is something that I have learnt to live with and though at times can be distress ing, the voices can often be re-assuring and affirming towards my own identity.

Since writing this Ben has changed his opinion slightly on the emphasis he was giving to DMT, telling me it was only one of his many concerns and that more needs to be understood about this phenomena.

Negative effects. The voices can be abusive or accusatory. They can give me a sense of dread or foreboding. I can lose consciousness. I can have visions of hideous and malformed faces and creatures. I suffer automaton feelings of being pushed, pulled and twisted. It is hard to walk sometimes and especially crossing the road. When this happens it can prove quite dangerous.

Positive Effects. The voices and visions can give me insight into metaphysical truths, be calming, loving, guiding and protective. I have 'Guardians'. They also strengthen my belief in God.

Vegan living

I had been getting interested in animal rights for a couple of years before becoming vegan. I was most concerned at the time with the ethical ramifications regarding animal testing and intensive farming practices. This was further intensified by watching a documentary about Pete Singers book on Ethics and his thoughts about 'humanocentric' (Pete Singers word) culture and reading about civilisations collapsing in America from intensive farming.

I was already primed with these ethical questions and I was thinking about becoming a vegetarian, when I had a nightmare (a really vivid waking nightmare) of being a terrified cow awaiting death in a slaughterhouse. I remembered the intense feeling a long while afterwards and decided I had to do something. Having already adopted my brother Sam's dietary restrictions (at his insistence that we all had food allergies and it wasn't just him) I had to skip vegetarianism and go straight to veganism. My issues with food intensified as I got more and more psychotic. I became upset at the thought of any lifeforms suffering and insisted on chopping vegetables with love, eating meals compassionately and returning peelings to the earth, much to the chagrin of the university staff residencies, as I was tipping the peelings out of the window. This should have sent a red flag warning to staff that I was most definitely unwell.

This concern for wellbeing then extended to the further harm I was doing to the earth with my big clumpy boots and the decision to take on the discomfort of being barefoot as a meditation on the world's pain.

Relationship with nature (development)

After deciding that church wasn't for me, there was the first sign that a psychosis would develop. I spent night after night with a white hole in my head and things reaching out through it. This was not an experience I'd had any preparation for and had no way to interpret it except through a christian filter and so I figured it was either Heaven or Hell trying to contact me. I was too afraid to interact with it directly, so I assumed it was offering a choice between being the Messiah or the Antichrist. I didn't want to be either of these, so I remained in crisis.

It was only after my mother bought me a book about Druidry and Celtic beliefs that this crisis abated and receded into the background. I always figured that by receiving that book I was being given permission to seek my own path.

I found it fascinating that Celtic ancestors worshipped nature and, as more news stories focused on possible global warming, species threatened with extinction, and industrial pollution, it didn't seem like a bad spiritual path. Of course this didn't really resolve my crisis, it just gave it pause. I was still desperate for answers and took stupid risks to get them.

Looking for Answers

Deciding to pursue Pagan rather than Christian beliefs did not mean that really fundamental questions had been answered. Venerating nature did not answer the questions: '*Is* there a God'? 'What is right or wrong?' or 'What the hell was that white light in my head?'

Whenever I played roleplaying games, I always wanted to be the wizard. Wizards were my favourite characters, so I made the dumb decision to see if I could become one in real life. There were lots of books on the subject and I liked to read; I still have a book on the Kabbala but the people in my head won't let me read it. They just put it back on the shelf and tell me I'm still on the 'water wings'

I got into meditation, not for finding inner peace, but to try and have 'out of body' experiences in psychic flight or get answers from the powers that be. I failed to get any out of body experiences, but banging on the walls of reality had an effect. Not the effect I really wanted, but I did get answers. How many of them were true or false is anybody's guess. But I sure as heck didn't know which were which, just drank it all up like a gullible idiot who thinks playing with magic doesn't have consequences.

Four Meditations

There are four meditations I conducted in a very unsafe manner, that had visionary results. These have been seared into my memory ever since and were conducted approximately one year before the big psychosis. Each one continues to resonate and each one fed into the 'big event'.

1. I may as well start with the most distressing. I was kneeling on the floor, eyes closed and I saw a mountain of skulls with a demon on the top. It reached out and pointing at me declared 'you're mine'. I was extremely distressed at this and had to work very hard to comfort my self. I sometimes wonder if this is the source of the regular experience as I'm drifting off to sleep of a malevolent (definitely male) force trying to rip the soul from my body. I cannot be sure but I've had these night terrors ever since coming round from the psychosis. Interestingly a female presence places a cold but reassuring hand upon my arm at these times and says, 'relax, everything will be fine' and then I go off to sleep shortly afterwards. I never see her face, her head is made entirely of light.

2. The second meditation was completely the opposite of the first. I was lying on my bed with my arms by my side breathing in and out deeply, calling out with my whole body. My arms still by my side felt as though they were crossed in the middle and I saw an angel. The angel did not look like anything I had read or seen. It was both massive and human sized at the same time. It bore two swords, one pointing upward and the other downwards. It was also in a wheel of fire. I asked who it was and it said 'Transformation'. I asked why it was here and it answered 'Transformation'. I asked what it wanted with me and it said again, 'Transformation' At this point I realised I wasn't going to get much conversation, so I replied rather churlishly 'Transform me then' and immediately it felt like my body was filled with fire. It was incredibly intense and I wondered whether it would ever stop. (Even

though it probably only lasted seconds, it felt timeless and uncomfortably present) but it was not unpleasant. I lay there thinking about what happened for a while and then just got on with the rest of the day. I have often considered this event as the true beginning of what was to come, but was it an angel or an instigator? I have never been in doubt that what I experienced was real, but have retained a number of unanswered questions. My foolish curiosity for getting them answered has not returned and I am happy to have these questions, doubts and puzzles remain as such.

3. The third meditation had no religious imagery, but hit at the very core of reality-perception. I was sat in my comfy chair, hands resting on my arms, again searching for an opening, to get some answers. Very rapidly the direction of the contact with the world changed and it was no longer *myself* in contact with the chair, but the chair in contact with *me*. I was being touched by an inanimate object as if I were an object. I jumped up disorientated and immediately sought to calm myself by burying my face into my duvet. But this gave me even greater distress as it was the duvet touching me. I panicked hoping that this would end soon (if at all) and tried shaking to myself out of it, by pacing up and down. I walked downstairs and one of my housemates said I looked like I'd seen a ghost. It was shortly after this that my attempts to hear the 'music of the spheres' (Pythagoras) started to bear fruit. Not an auspicious start, but an essential part of the journey and not one I regret in hindsight.

4. The final meditation was just a few months before going to University and was really quite prophetic. I was once again meditating, in my comfy chair, going deeper and deeper into myself, down as far as I could dare to go. I heard a voice asking if I'd like to be a Werewolf and they made it seem like a perfectly fine thing to be, not at all dangerous. My mind answered yes without really thinking about it and then the voice became less friendly when it said 'fine'. I was gripped then by something close to my core and gripped also by fear, as I had not realised what I'd agreed to and the ramifications. I was greatly worried by the tone of the voice, which sounded like a business man concluding a deal and not one I felt I could trust. I put it all to one side and comforted myself with the thought that I was just being silly and that nothing really happened. No deal had been made, etc. After I started to become

animals, I remembered the meditation. I remembered the warning at the core of my being, but I was free of the pain of being human, so I wasn't paying too much attention to warnings - too busy having fun.

For many years after coming back from psychosis I avoided meditation, as I could see its role in getting me to a place I could not easily return from. Something I've learned to be wary of and to be much clearer in my motivation to practice it. Prometheus paid a price for stealing from the gods and I learned to my cost that theft is still frowned upon when Spider revoked my 'licence to fly' and became my rather harsh mentor.

The Great Music

After smoking some cannabis, I became extremely distressed, because I looked out of the window and realised that I would never make music as beautiful as the wind through the trees and their essential harmony with the birds. And then I realised that birds were far superior musicians than I ever would be and without needing to try. The intensity was such that I was inconsolable.

This was the day Sam shouted at me when I was in the shower room at Wellow, 'You're a f***ing schizophrenic you are!' This was long before I got diagnosed but in some ways I was glad someone did notice where I was heading, even if they weren't really helping the situation.

I had become obsessed with Pythagoras' 'Music of the Spheres' and the Celtic concept of the Oran Mor 'The Great Music' of humanity, nature and existence. After the distress of this first experience I realised that I desperately wanted to hear that music and felt it would complete my soul.

I tried extending my thoughts into the cosmos to see if I could hear the psychic song of the moon, sun and anything at all. After the meditation which reversed 'contacting' direction, this became much easier. I'm not sure if I ever heard moon (I convinced myself that I did) but I did start hearing the trees and the tarmac. Oh God! The Tarmac! I couldn't shift my attention from it, all I could hear was the stone in torment, torment, compounded whenever a car went past. And the cars seemed so present, so real and malevolent. I was practising with 'inner ears' more and more, but it was always coming back to that b***** tarmac.

I began to realise that people held themselves in tension, like they were made of strings and if I tuned my inner ear, I could hear the vibration of them: solo, trio, quartet, an interaction beyond speaking, life as a grand symphony. I tried writing what I was hearing, but I lacked the compositional skill and just ended up writing random marks on manuscript paper in crayon, trying to make sense of it. I was definitely hearing more, but I kept going back to the tarmac.

I could hear the rhythm of the broken air-conditioning in the refectory. I could hear the birdsong-like melody of private conversations at my table and the harmonic drone of all the other conversations echoing. But I always went back to the tarmac and it was slowly destroying me.

I still hear with my 'inner ear' but I'm less prone to drowning in it and can tune in or out more or less at will now. It feels somewhat like using my brain as a 'ping pong' bat bouncing consciousness off objects and listening with invisible ears.

It is the greatest gift that psychosis has ever given me. Not sure it was worth the price but being able to hear the song of nature and my own part in it is truly wondrous. It feels like a language that binds all things together and that it is our duty to be harmonious in the great cosmic orchestra.

The side effect is getting disoriented in the visually loud environment, ceaselessly shouting without a single thought about the effect it has on the psyche. An effect which I believe is felt even when people cannot actively 'hear' like I do.

This is a primeval kind of language used long before what we now understand as universal language.

Shapeshifting

I remember walking on my tiptoes when I was a young child and my elder brother, worried that I was play acting the wearing of high heels, would clip me round the back of my head. He was trying to make me more 'manly'.

I was actually play acting being a horse. I figured that because they seem to walk on tiptoes, they were better runners and I wanted to be a better runner (I also wanted to be a Mini Metro).

Behaving like a horse, was my first animal, but not yet as a transformation.

I had a really vivid dream of a giant spider on my ceiling and became very afraid of spiders afterwards. We were living in Wallingford at the time, so I must have been quite young. I like to think that it was 'spider' introducing herself for the first time and me, being a kid, completely misinterpreted the greeting.

It was probably just a vivid dream, but Horse, Spider, and Mini Metro have all been significant to me as an adult.

I first felt the call (to shapeshift) while sitting in Sociology class. I would sit there enjoying the lecture, but this feeling of compulsion to jump through the window and run wild like an animal. I never gave in to it (of course) but it was so strong that I could hear my bestial roar banging on the door of my brain. I was really into Paganism at this point and I had begun find out about shapeshifting as a practice. I read about tribal cultures with animal totems and hunting rituals that called upon animal spirits. I began to see animal transformation not as a werwolf 'curse' but the very root of human spirituality. I wanted 'in'. I wanted a totem animal; I wanted to become like some African or North American Shaman.

Sometimes you should be careful what you wish for.

This is pretty much the case with my shapeshifting. To do it safely requires training and discipline. I had cannabis and a desire to be free of being me, lots of books with potentially dangerous ideas in them, and not much caution. So it was always going to end badly.

Of course when it happened it was by accident rather than by design. Having been romantically rejected yet again, I became despondent and convinced that humanity was rarely humane.

I walked into the middle of a shallow river, got on my knees and very solemnly rejected my humanity.

Emotional stress and a head full of Pagan mythology multiplied by a bad reaction to cannabis equals a wish granted. A few days later I started to leave reality when I began to bark.

Dog was my first transformation and I absolutely loved it: I was free. I was wild. Then came Crow, an equally powerful embodiment. I would point at danger with my stick and 'caw'. I felt like a harbinger standing upon a rock, dancing with the trees, as rooks flew overhead in a figure of eight motion. What heaven!

Then came Spider spinning me round and round. Spinning as I walked, spinning up and down stairs. Spinning as I sat (rotating onto my head and then back round again, over and over). I became a dancing Monkey. Being spun into the web, like Fly, full of corruption that needs to be drawn out. I viewed this web of the Spider as a safety net that stopped me falling further.

And then Dog returned, but now he seemed sickly and corrupted. Voices began proclaiming me a manifestation of the Hound of God, beyond the morality of humanity. Humanity were my natural prey, they said, and that was when it stopped being fun any more. I found myself fighting this voice, but with little humanity left after all these transformations, the struggle against this evil was like a bitter life and death battle played out repeatedly.

The Moles came to me then. My head was underground with them as they put their claws to their lips in a hushing motion and pointed at a root that they told me was my tap root. I must be careful not to break it, they said or my soul would die. If I had given into the evil voice it would have and I would be lost forever. I kept fighting, though the hallucinations were now everything and everywhere.

Spider returned but not to spin me. She came in all her dread, a force that I could not deny. I was in her web, I had been spun and there was now no escaping my fate.

I came to realise that we are all in the web and that our words and deeds have untold consequences. Mine had summoned Spider and she was most displeased. I had played with things I should not and I must pay the price. She became Queen Spider to me then, putting me right. But I had to be dissolved first.

A painful process which others call a schizophrenic episode, was for me a confusing rearrangement of beliefs and perceptions.

Queen Spider still lives in my head, I look and see the webwork, but I am careful not to attract her attention. She is powerful, dangerous, and terrifying but she is not evil. I see her as the embodiment of fate that judges, but her judgement can be averted if we but learn to dance with the Great Music.

I had broken so many rules, that now I was being forced to see and hear. At times I still get trapped in her 'cage' of consequences, terrified of breaking reality, terrified of reality breaking me.

But this wisdom is the kind that I must be clothed in, not just espouse. It cuts to the core.

I have learnt that animals will come and go. I am not to summon them; I am not to hold onto them; I must let them drift in and out. They each have a lesson.

The only one who has stayed full time is Dog and he now barks a warning, 'Don't go inside, it is not your place, get out, get out, get out.' All this is conveyed with a single bark. He is long suffering, probably resents me, but has kept me safe one way or another. I should probably take him out for walks but instead I hide in my rabbit hole.

Crow returned during the big psychosis. I was building castles in the sky, trying to create a psychic friends and family network to communicate telepathically without getting into trouble. Crow flew into my head and said, 'I am *not* your friend. I am certainly *not* your family. I am a harbinger.' Crow flew off. I stopped building castles that day.

I had been told.

He has occasionally re-appeared over the years, always after a falling out with someone or when I have let something go. I'm glad he's there, no matter how curmudgeonly he is.

And Horse? Horse was one of the two animals that I was transformed into most recently. Yet another social defeat featuring cruelty, or manipulation, knocked me out of commission. But the Hebrew patriarch guided and counselled me and Spider worked in tandem to ride me like a horse. I didn't get into trouble they just rode me to the shops and back, cooked me dinner, and sat comforting me. I was at that time on 'short reins'. But they were keen for me to ride myself again as soon as possible (long reins). The longer they rode me the more 'doll like' I became afterwards and they wished me no harm like this. When I was ready they left me to it and I stayed 'doll like' for severals weeks. During this time I became Earthworm and understood that all life, no matter how evolved it is, is at its heart a time worm. Time passes through us and is transformed and we are transformed by time itself into shapes that we could not have predicted. Doll-like I consumed my time until I could ride myself once more.

Is it bad that I miss being on a short reins? No freedom, sure, but also no danger. But I have learnt that transformations come and go. They have an appointed hour, they have a purpose and they contain hard wisdom that must be digested.

<u>The Mini Metro</u>

During my psychosis an authoritative voice said, 'Some souls are like bicycles, some are like cars. Yours is an articulated lorry and you've just jack-knifed.' I was told to get in the back, ride my bicycle and they would teach me how to drive. Never has a more profound realisation been given to me like that. As if handed out like a 'chugger' [charity mugger] hands out a pamphlet.

This communication has informed my journey towards recovery like no other.

I now know I was never a bicycle. I was never a Mini Metro (no matter how much I wanted to be one as a child). I was an out of control juggernaut and nobody had taught me how to drive, because they assumed that learning how to ride a bike or drive a small 'putt-putt' would suffice.

Schizophrenia is not, in my opinion, a disease but rather a complex experience that requires training. Expert training to avoid crashing.

Psychosis is the end result of not training how to manage the experience.

Me being ridden around like a horse by voices did not result in psychosis, because I am more aware of the procedures necessary to avert catastrophe. Becoming a Dog, a Spider, then a Monkey, then a Dog again *did* result in psychosis. I didn't know how to be safe and clung onto the experience until it sickened and then made me sick.

I always wanted to be Mini Metro, but you can't always get what you want.

Some of us get to be Space Ships where it's much harder to check your mirror and signals: lots of buttons.

The difference is the amount of experience I've had in learning how to manage it.

Surely it would have been better to have these driving lessons before I got 'Illthy'?

Ben did eventually try one more time to study, but this proved too much of a strain on his inner life. So with great sadness wrote this letter explaining his reason for leaving the degree course.

College of Life and Environmental Sciences
University of Exeter
EX4 4QG

27August 2012

Dear Dr. C

I would like to thank you for all the support you gave me during my time studying, especially when I was struggling to remain focused during the 2nd year. It was a very difficult time and your patient counsel was much appreciated.

In the last 8 months, I have been recuperating and considering my options. At each turn the thought of returning to study became increasingly fraught with doubts and concerns about maintaining my health. It has been difficult to accept, but the rigours of studying such a complex subject have had a negative impact on my mental health that was not immediately apparent at the time.

Whilst the anxiety attacks have now diminished to a degree that is now bearable, the underlying cause of them remains. It has taken a long time to realise that each time I sat down to write an essay, I was coming too close to a place that I have an overwhelming fear of and each time the effort of retaining control was becoming harder. This has been a huge personal disappointment, yet it has also helped me to understand with greater poignancy, that recovery is much more than the appearance of 'normality' under normal circumstances.

I am very sorry that I am unable to continue with the course, as I feel that I have not only let myself down, but also those (like yourself) who provided such wonderful support and encouragement. I have not lost my interest in psychology, nor have I given up on achieving full recovery, but I have reached the conclusion that until such time that I can safely inhabit internal space, it is better to seek a path that keeps me focused primarily on the external world. I do not know fully where I am headed as yet, but I remain optimistic that the answers I am looking for will be found.

Warmest regards,

Ben Durkin

8

Correspondence Regarding Ben's Mental Health Care

This chapter contains various letters and statements over a wide range of time to show how much intervention was necessary to protect him from complicated situations getting out of control. Many of the instances for my complaints were due entirely to poor attitudes towards Ben as the recipient of the 'care' and a total lack of respect to us as a family.

Many of the problems arising could have been avoided if the people who were considered the professionals had just engaged more constructively with Ben and us instead of justifying their positions after the event.

Ben's progress was seriously hampered by such behaviour during these stressful times, so I was unable to take these matters further and was left with a sense of powerlessness. In the face of what was seen then, the authorities and professionals held the attitude that only they, not us working with them, should determine Ben's future course.

I sincerely hope that the situation has improved for anyone needing these particular services at present.

Many times a 'carer' will find themselves intervening on behalf of the person needing care. Nowadays I believe that there is better support available for families. However by my including these letters and statements, you may understand just how much time was taken up with the administration side of caring for Ben.

The following extract of a letter I wrote dated April 2000 was to the Ivybridge doctor, whose proposed outcomes of treatment were never fully explained. We had to cease the visits due to the mounting costs and our feeling disappointed with the results:

> We requested a test to ascertain his food allergies in particular. He claimed to be allergic to yeast. I had always maintained that his 'vegan' stance was a product of his mental state and that his avoidance of certain foods was because of some psychological abhorrence rather than an actual allergy. I just wanted some testing done to either confirm or refute my theory. However we did not receive any fully comprehensive testing and the majority of the consultation seemed to be devoted to his 'energy fields'.
>
> As the cost of caring for him has escalated and he has still yet to be accepted for any benefits, we have to cease our visits to your clinic.
>
> He is now back to eating a full and varied diet that includes meat, fish, fresh fruit and vegetables and yes, even bread, and products containing yeast, such as beer. All to no ill effect. He is still unable to study, read or concentrate for very long and is often jittery and has bouts of being 'tormented'.
>
> However, since we took him away with us on a cruise this winter his spirits have generally been a lot brighter.
>
> Much of what he has achieved in these recent months has been due to patience and perseverance on the part of his family and medical intervention. I am still not quite sure what he gained from your treatment, except perhaps to acknowledge to himself how he needed to change his lifestyle.
>
> The cranial osteopathy sessions you recommended certainly gave him a boost. He believes that some cognitive therapy would help rather than the anti-psychotic drugs he has to take. I shall investigate this possibility.
>
> I hope this letter will be of interest to you. I am sure you like to know the outcome of clients who do not return, if only for your records.

Having enjoyed a wonderful week cruising in the Caribbean in February it was recommended and authorised by his CPN that Ben could also enjoy some relaxation and fun with others nearer his own age at a respite care centre in the New Forest near

Southampton. This would also give me a chance to have a break from caring for a while and re-charge my energy.

Ben and I visited the place together before booking to make sure that he would feel comfortable with this arrangement. It all seemed very friendly and it was not far from where his brother Sam was living, so that would give them an opportunity for meeting up.

All seemed to go well, the date for early May was booked and the itinerary sounded interesting. It was advertised as a Multi-cultural week offering an evening with a steel band, Caribbean and Asian food, African music and visits to cultural centres with religious needs catered for.

Oh dear how wrong can one be?

This precious week turned into a nightmare for Ben, who was just so relieved when we collected him and brought him back home. It was a total disaster as regards respite, either for us or him and took us all some time to recover.

For a start the 'Caribbean' programme, unknown to us, had been cancelled. The reason given was, 'There were not enough takers for the event.' The age range of people staying tended to be older than Ben and some of them were severely disturbed. One middle-aged woman in particular followed Ben around all week describing to to him, in graphic detail, how she had killed all her children. Ben spent two of the days escaping to his brother's, as he hated the place so much. The food was mediocre and the social events were of a kind one would expect in a poorly run institution for the elderly.

Ben, being a polite young man, just went along with it all rather than complain.

We then spent a harrowing few months wrangling over the costs of this 'special week', as the organisers had not fulfilled their side of the contract and had not allowed us a 'let out' when they drastically changed, or rather cancelled, the programme of events.

The sheer number of letters written to and fro regarding the costs and appalling care that Ben received would take far too much space. It was not until October - five months later that we eventually had our complaints addressed and a short letter of apology from their Credit Control Manager. She decided to write off the

£25 they had claimed was still owing. We never received any apology from the respite centre staff or managers.

Still reeling from this ill-fated encounter with the National Schizophrenia Fellowship (NSF) whose mission strap line at the time was 'positive response to mental illness' we encountered a further shock on receiving a letter (see next page) this time banning our son from activities at a day centre he had regularly been attending. This was due to a disastrous and poorly managed outing to Bath, Somerset the same month.

We had all been a bit apprehensive about Ben going on this outing but he was persuaded that it would be beneficial and he would be accompanied by those who were trained in assisting people with mental health needs.

The first we knew of any problem on the outing, was when Ben received the following letter.

The plan had been, for the whole group at the Old Bakery to take a coach trip to the city of Bath. I think this was intended to be a cultural and social outing with enough carers travelling in the party to accommodate the needs of these variously vulnerable people.

However, certain members of the group were well known to drink too much and mix and match drugs with each other so a special watch should have been set up to prevent these individuals getting isolated from the main group.

Our trust in the management of such an outing by professionals who should have been aware of certain possible problems arising, evaporated, as you will see from the following statement.

Bath Trip 24th May 2000. The statement of Mrs. M. Durkin written on 3rd June 2000 and which includes Ben's account.

Dear Sirs,

As I was not informed about this banning before it occurred by any of the people in charge of this service. It came as a great shock. Especially the way it was administered.

Benjamin has told me that there was no personal consultation with him prior to the ban, just a 'dressing down' in the company of the other person banned. This was done on two occasions and Ben felt unable to speak up in his defence with the other person

nsf Tiverton District Day Services
The Old Bakery,
44 Westexe South,
Tiverton, Devon.
EX16 5DH
Phone & Fax 01884 254425

positive response to mental illness **nsf**

7th June 2000

PRIVATE AND CONFIDENTIAL

Ben Durkin
The Old Bakery
5 Fore Street
Uffculme
Cullompton
Devon

Dear Ben Durkin

As a result of your behaviour during the trip to Bath on Wednesday 24th May the decision has been made to exclude you from day services for a period of one calendar month. This period of exclusion started on Thursday June 1st 2000 and ends on Friday 30th June.

The need for you to behave appropriately is an important aspect of your use of day services. The reason for your exclusion is as follows:-

1.) That you drunk more than two alcoholic drinks during your visit to Bath. It was clearly explained to you that the no drink rule had been relaxed on that day and members could if they wish have up to two alcoholic drinks.

2.) The use of day services while using or intoxicated on non prescribed drugs (including illegal drugs and substances) is a clear ground for exclusion. You have admitted that you used illegal drugs during the visit to Bath. This is a clear breach of the policy.

I point out that your use of drugs could have had serious legal implications for you and for staff members and I if we were seen to act in a way which ignored your behaviour on the trip to Bath.

The exclusion policy states that anyone excluded from the Project can only normally regain membership after a review meeting has been held with that person's keyworker. I will ask [redacted], project worker, to contact your key worker to arrange a review meeting with you and your key worker at the end of your period of exclusion. I enclose a copy of the exclusion policy for your information.

Your keyworker has been informed of this action.

Yours sincerely

[redacted]

Project Manager

key worker

CC [redacted] Tiverton CMHT Leigh House.
CC [redacted] NSF Locality Manager
CC [redacted], NSF Operations Manager

National Schizophrenia Fellowship exists to help people with severe mental illness, their families and carers.

President: Professor J K Wing CBE
Chairperson: Cecil Kavanagh MBE
Chief Executive: Cliff Prior

Tel: 0181-547 3937
Fax: 0181-547 3826
Advice line: 0181-974 6814
Internet: www.nsf.org.uk
email: info@nsf.org.uk

NSF is a company limited by guarantee, registered in England number 1227970. Registered charity number 271028.

Registered Office: 28 Castle Street Kingston-upon-Thames Surrey KT1 1SS

present. He was not told whether an incident form had been completed or that he could appeal .

On the day in question, Ben has told me that he did not want to be alone in a strange city, and he thought being with people he regarded as friends, would be better than going it alone. At D's suggestion they went to a pub. (I believe this was the first error of judgement Ben made.) I also have been told that it was J who was given the mobile phone number to make contact with the 'carers'. (This information should have been available to each individual.) These carers did not question this little group of three, as to where they might be going, when everyone else in 2000 party set off for coffee.

One of the carers should have made it their priority to oversee this breakaway group. I believe it was at this point that serious professional error of judgement occurred in not accompanying them to the pub and quietly coaxing them all to do something more interesting.

J had told Ben he'd taken some of D's sleeping tablets the night before just to see what they were like, then he offered some roll-ups around and Ben lit up and discovered he was smoking a rather thin 'spliff' but continued to finish it and accepted no more. Both D and Ben stayed with J drinking, but they were becoming increasingly bothered by J's behaviour.(Remember J had already taken someone else's medication, as well as his own, he had continued to smoke his own roll-ups and was now drinking heavily). Ben has told me that things were sort of OK up to about lunchtime, and whilst D was still around. D could see this situation was fast getting out of control and urged Ben to leave with him for a bus tour of the city. Ben was also getting more anxious and wanted to leave, but also was concerned about J's condition which was deteriorating faster now and was worried about how J would get back to the coach. He felt he had no option but sit it out.

D left Ben with J saying he would return. He did not. Ben was by now becoming desperate to persuade a very unruly J to stop drinking and move on. He completely lost track of time during this stress and when he did realise how late it was he was already unable to cope with J who had by now fallen on the floor. Ben tried lifting him up and J then fell on top of him dead drunk and totally out-of-it. Ben struggled to get the drink, J was holding, out of his hand, but J insisted on taking it outside with him and then smashed the glass in the street. This made Ben even more embarrassed and scared of the consequences. He then lost his bearings and could not locate the coach station until very much later.

He could not possibly have got J back to the coach, if, as accused, he had been drunk himself. The behaviour of J on entering the coach and the whole journey back was disgraceful and again Ben was left struggling to control his friend by putting out lit cigarettes and preventing him from singing. At no time did any of the so-called carers come to Ben's assistance but condemned him by association. It was Ben's calmness despite his distress that prevented a much uglier situation occurring.

D who had taken part in the days events had already returned to the coach.

Re J: The day following this incident he left a message of apology on our answerphone to Ben, for his appalling behaviour. His CPN has also been informed of the potential problems with this young man. This in no way excuses Ben's intake that day but gives a wider view of the context of these events and their tragic outcome.

It seems that association with this person has meant that Ben has not been either seen nor treated as an individual in his own right. There was a third party involved with them at the beginning of the day and throughout, who managed to escape banning because he decided he'd had enough of J's behaviour and left. This meant he was not present when the time came to extract an extremely drunken and uncontrollable J out of the pub and back to the coach station.

Ben was not too keen to go on this trip but had been persuaded by JB at Club 2000 that it would be good to go and he need not worry immediately about the money needed.

I have for a long time had serious reservations about J. We have had to warn him about illegal substances and I have on several occasions voiced my concerns to J's parents. I had also informed Ben's CPN of the potential problem situation and informed him that through the influence of J, Ben may become embroiled again in the very things he is trying so hard to avoid.

Whilst on the phone to JB on Friday 2nd June, I was told that they are all adults and responsible for their own behaviour alone. Well, I accept the fact that they are all adults but if they are able to manage their daily affairs without support then why have they all been referred to such a support group with supervision, if it is not an essential requirement?

I am utterly appalled that Ben should have been left in charge of someone so out of control, and then castigated for being in his company. All three had drunk more than the allotted amount. However I am told it was because of the terrible behaviour on the coach and the late arrival back, that Ben is banned. Ben would not have been late if he had left with D. He would not have been with J and therefore would not have been associated with J's disgusting episode.

We have witnesses who will be willing to speak on Ben's behalf that he was trying desperately to control the situation and was at his wits end. This whole affair has affected Ben very badly and he has been so depressed that I have only just been able to coax out of him the whole story. He is not perfect, we know that and he has many personal weaknesses and is easily led. But had I thought that this outing would have turned into such a terrible nightmare, I would never have let him go. I thought he would be in the company of people who cared about him.

Benjamin is in an extremely vulnerable position and I have personally nursed him since his collapse at University last June. That is why this is all the more serious for us as a family, because we have coped for a long while without support. These care centre activities have not only been a life-line to our son but a respite for me.

My husband works away in London all week on a permanent basis and I am also caring for his very elderly mother who will not accept she needs more help. I am now seriously considering whether Ben should ever return to a group whose carers are so ready to denounce clients without first hearing the whole story.

I would appreciate an early response to this letter.

Thank you.

I have included this letter as an example of how easily Ben could be drawn into others' bad behaviour and get the blame for subsequent problems. He has a strong sense of justice and a will to assist others, despite any personal misgivings. He would never abandon anyone he felt was in a vulnerable state.

This situation became absolutely intolerable and to this day no proper apology has ever been forthcoming on the outcome to Ben's wrongful banishment and lack of due care to himself from those in authority.

The next letter I received from the locality manager was extremely long and basically focused entirely on the alcohol and illegal drug use. Both of which Ben had explained in his statement how he had at first taken a cigarette that was offered, before realising what it was and that he could not have been drunk to such an extent, if he was able to get the 'friend' back onto the coach. This man clearly did not see that the breach of their care policy to such vulnerable and troubled individuals was of much greater moral concern.

The following letter I sent, also complains about the methods they used to deal with those involved:

Locality Manager
NSF Sentapoint
2, Bank Place,
Market Street
Crediton EX17 2AJ

20th June 2000

re: Your letter of 16th June

Dear Mr. D,

We have just received your letter of 16th June 2000 regarding our son Ben. It was not addressed to Mr. & Mrs. Durkin, but hand written to 'The Old Bakery'. This is really not acceptable considering the confidentiality of the contents. It is also extremely impolite not to address us personally.

We see from your letter that you have not satisfactorily answered the points listed in our letter of the 13th June 2000. We are complaining about the manner in which this business has been handled.

We consequently feel that because you persist in referring only to our son's alcohol consumption and the illegal substance smoked, to which he has clearly confessed, we have no other option but to take this matter further.

You have completely disregarded the way this ban was imposed, and the actions of the carers on this trip and the lack of a full investigation about others involved.

We totally disagree with you that if Ben had returned to the coach alone he would still have been banned. The other person in this small group was D, who had himself drunk more than the limit allowed and used the same illegal substance, which came from J. As far as we are aware he has never been questioned and therefore not banned. Ben would not have been questioned either if he had returned with D. We will persist in making this point to show how little care was taken to discover the whole truth.

It is a matter of principle to us, not whether Ben was 'guilty' of any offence.

We have still heard nothing from any one on the staff to alleviate our worries. It quite clearly states in your complaints procedure that both a written and verbal reply is given within three days. Your letter dated 16th June was not posted until 9 pm on 19th June.

We feel that this shows us a lack of respect and urgency.

We do not ordinarily spend our time complaining but are deeply concerned about the attitude towards clients and their family, in this situation.

We have enclosed a full report from Ben of what took place that day.

Yours sincerely.

Mr. & Mrs. M. Durkin

Copies will be sent to the local Ombudsman, Director of NSF, and CPN.

The final letter in this affair was a reasonable, if rather diluted assessment of the situation, towards the end of what had been an upsetting experience. Ben did return to the day centre, for a short period afterwards, but his attendance was sporadic, as not surprisingly the enthusiasm he once felt had gone.

I believe now that the NSF has since changed its name to Rethink Mental Illness.

Interestingly it's new strap line is the reverse of the old one 'changing attitudes, changing lives'. It used to read 'changing lives, changing attitudes'!

A great deal of my time was taken up with the huge amount of administrative tasks needed to keep Ben's care working smoothly.

The Sentapoint Project

positive response to mental illness **nsf** Operations

The Old Bakery
5 fore Street
Uffculme
Devon
EX15 3AN

21st June 2000

Dear Mr & Mrs Durkin,

I received your response to my letter dated the 16th June. I am sorry that you feel that I have not addressed the issues you have raised to your satisfaction.

In view of this I have passed all relevant paperwork etc to my Manager, [redacted], Operations Manager for Somerset, Devon & Cornwall, for her consideration in the hope that this matter may be resolved.

Regards

[redacted]

(Locality Manager)

National Schizophrenia Fellowship exists to help people with severe mental illness, their families and carers.

President: Cecil Kavanagh MBE
Chairperson: Jenny Fisher
Chief Executive: Cliff Prior

Tel: 01363 774737
Fax: 01363 776030
Advice Line: 0181 974 6814
Internet: www.nsf.org.uk

NSF is a company limited by guarantee, registered in England number 1227970
Registered charity number 271028

NSF
Sentapoint
2 Bank Place
Market Street
Crediton
EX17 2AJ

changing lives, changing attitudes

positive response to mental illness

nsf

Operations

Mr & Mrs Durkin
The Old Bakery
5 Fore Street
Uffculme
Devon
EX15 3AN

30th June 2000.

Dear Mr & Mrs Durkin,

I have been forwarded copies of the various letters sent by yourselves with regard to Ben's temporary exclusion from the NSF Tiverton Day Service and also the responses made by NSF staff.

I can fully appreciate how difficult this situation has been for you and understand your frustration at the perceived process. It is obviously important that this matter is fully and openly discussed and that if the process was not correctly implemented or Ben or yourselves were disadvantaged by it that we do something to address this and to ensure that a better process is implemented in the future.

In his letter of 26th June, [redacted], NSF Locality Manager, offered to meet with you to discuss your views and thoughts on what happened and I do feel that this would be beneficial especially as [redacted] has now had further opportunity to talk with the staff from the Tiverton project.

If you feel it would be useful for me to be part of this meeting I would be very happy to attend, equally you may wish to include [redacted].

If you would prefer not to meet but would like the matter pursued by means of a formal investigation then obviously I will undertake this or indeed we could meet and then still agree that a more formal investigation needs to take place.

Whichever way we proceed I would like to assure you that the matter has been taken seriously. We will be reviewing the way our services respond to these types of incidents to ensure that we try at all times to act in the

National Schizophrenia Fellowship exists to help people with severe mental illness, their families and carers.

President [illegible] Chairperson [illegible] Chief Executive [illegible]

Tel: 01823 354879
Fax: 01823 354885
Advice Line: 0181 974 6814
Internet: www.nsf.org.uk
Email: [illegible]

NSF is a company limited by guarantee, registered in England number 1227970. Registered charity number 271028

Reply to:
NSF, 2 The Crescent
Taunton, Somerset
TA1 4EA

best interests of the people who use our services, their carers, our staff and the general public. I accept that this is never an easy task, especially when we also have to consider the law and the consequences of individual behaviour on others.

However your complaint has raised serious issues and as such they will be tackled and I hope constructively resolved.

Yours sincerely,

[redacted]

Operations Manager.

Operations Manager
NSF, 2 The Crescent
Taunton, Somerset
TA1 4EA

4th July 2000

Dear Ms. G,

Thank you for your letter of 30th June 2000.
As it is now a full month since I raised concerns with J B at the 'Old Bakery' Tiverton, we feel that due to the passage of time, the accuracy of the memories of all concerned will have faded.

With regard to H D's letter of the 16th June (correct date). If you refer to it, you will see that no real attempt to meet was offered in the last bulleted paragraph, where he would seem to be implying that there were no grounds as far as he could see for an appeal, to be relevant. He uses such ambiguous language. He, like Mr B seem unable to really listen to what we had clearly underlined in our correspondence. We feel that talking to either him or JB now, would just end in their defending their actions and we left feeling frustrated again .

S F (CPN) is now on holiday, his contribution has been invaluable. We would indeed, have wanted him to be present as well, as an independent mediator. But the time lapse would be more than six weeks and this will not solve matters that have long since passed.

Had we received some assurance from the beginning, that a thorough investigation had been conducted and the subsequent correct actions taken, we would not have felt it necessary to continue with our complaint.

We therefore ask that more stringent procedures be implemented to investigate future problems and greater emphasis placed on justifiable and confidential communication between an individual and those in authority. Also that all clients have access to the mobile phone numbers of carers when out in groups. We request that it be recorded that it is only because there is nowhere else, at present for Ben to receive day-care or a Club for his age group, that he will return to the services from which he was banned.

Mrs M Durkin

By now there were less visits from CPN's, still no NHS CBT and a general lack of care and attention to the effects that the prescribed drugs were having on his general physical health.

We began a new venture of looking for more intellectually stimulating pursuits. I booked us both in for a talk at the Dartington Book Festival that summer.

Not all my letters were those of complaint or request.

The Hearing Voices Network had become such a prominent feature of Ben's wellbeing that we wanted those in the Exeter branch especially, to know how much they were appreciated.

From those first very tentative steps into this new environment where Ben was accepted and not considered 'strange' we were able to trust those who truly worked for the benefit of others. So I wrote them a letter of appreciation:

Andrew Barkla and Claire
HVN Joan of Arc Room
Exeter

25th October 2002

What the Hearing Voices Network in Exeter has meant to a carer.

It has taken me some time to commit to print what this Group has meant to our son, us and me in particular. That is not because I have no tangible proof of the benefits received, it is due more to how I find the right words to describe our relief at finding that such a place existed.

We had been struggling along with the barest of 'community support' that was for the most part totally inadequate for the needs of those who attended, especially if they had more than one brain cell.

From Ben's first tentative beginnings with HVN Exeter; when he was unsure about what might be expected of him or how he would fit in with the existing members, he has changed radically, to the present time when he enthusiastically joins in with seminars. He is actively involved with the Experts by Experience group, and the confidence that he has gained working with various mental health professionals has aided his personal recovery. This has been due to the incredible hard work and support offered by Andrew and Claire mainly and the many others, who encourage people like Ben.

This place and this amazing group of people all with different needs and aspirations has enabled Ben to rejoin society as a useful and worthy contributor instead of someone who just receives 'care in the community' with its narrow perspectives and despicable lack of funding.

He has been able to contribute to the support and encouragement of others, even though he still suffers from the effects of his illness and occasionally has to take a back seat. The warm acceptance of each person's need for respite and recovery as they contribute, allows people to feel appreciated and respected in a way that much of today's so called 'caring' society does not.

I wholeheartedly support this work. The organisers, whose tireless efforts are often rewarded only with the enormous benefits they see gained by those who attend, should be given a higher status in the well-being of the mentally ill. These people are doing an

> extremely important job for society by giving back the power to cope and the hope of recovery to those who would otherwise be disregarded and even despised.
>
> I was in despair when we first attended this place, wondering if this was going to become just another 'dead-end' where Ben felt ill at ease. But I have seen such a transition in our son in the past eighteen months that it can only be due to the general attitude and philosophy of those who help and attend the groups sessions. A very big THANK YOU goes to everyone involved.
>
> The spirit of 'Joan of Arc' lives on, terrifying the powerful bureaucratic attitude to sanity, by accepting that one who hears voices may have deeper insight, and perhaps more to contribute, than those who ignore the validity of this experience.

I assisted in some of the artistic workshops held in this place and enjoyed contributing to the meaningful and creative processes happening in the lives of those who attended.

Due to other pressing family commitments I sadly had to discontinue my connection with the Joan of Arc group when it changed to become The Bridge Collective C.I.C and moved from its original premises to the present day rooms in King Street Business Centre, Exeter.

Ben also left for a while as he had undergone some setbacks in his treatment and was unable to cope with the organisational side of the group.

However he is now back, and very much involved with what is happening and regularly attends meetings and organises fund raising events.

9

Professionals and Medication versus 'Client' and Family?

'The light is reached not by turning back from the darkness, but by going through it.'

Leonard Roy Frank

I have added a question mark to my chapter heading because I would hope by now that this situation no longer exists, where one is made to feel in conflict with or inferior due to not being a 'professional'.

I understand that not all families want to, or can be closely involved with assisting the outcomes of treatment for their family member. In some cases there may be disagreements within the family, that would just exacerbate the sufferer's torments.

Yet, when families do want to help, I believe this should always be encouraged, even if sometimes it can be a bit overwhelming to begin with, for all concerned. If taken at a steady pace, allowing each person some time to express their own understanding of the current situation, a sense of trust can be developed.

Rather than the confrontational attitude that we mostly endured, the professionals could include the family unit as a positive support framework in which continued treatment is administered with the client's agreement. A process of building group confidence this way could outweigh any perceived 'non professional' input from family members and thus address the sense of abandonment often felt by the 'patient'.

By March 2000, I had been asked to fill in a form to establish that I was Ben's main carer. This was supposed to open the door to a local support group for me. Unfortunately this did not work out very well, partly owing to the fact that the meetings were held in the same building from which Ben was later banned. The format was arranged as group meetings, with little opportunity to speak privately about one's needs or concerns. Also one of the first speakers invited, was the Psychiatrist who had continually demanded that Ben be admitted to hospital for treatment. So I just made use of another care support worker that I was entitled to because I was also caring for my mother-in-law. The help and advice I received from this person was invaluable. I shall always be grateful that I had someone other than family in which to confide .

Sometimes having a family member or close friend write a statement about the person for whom help is sought, can be a way of painting a wider picture of the whole person rather than just viewing the 'illness'. This could identify opportunities to engage more creatively with them once they begin to communicate coherently.

I knew that once he was living more independently, he might need some personal historical facts to inform the mental health team of his life before psychosis. Information not necessarily on his file, as it came from his family's perspective. So I wrote the following statement in support of our son Ben.

1999-2003

Ben became severely ill during the spring term of his first year at Lampeter University. During the preceding months he had shown an increasing tendency to bizarre appearance and eccentric mannerisms and ideas. We attributed this at first, as a desire to be different, to stand out from the crowd or impress.

When he previously attended South Downs College in Hampshire, to study modern music, he was considered by the head of the department as a possible Oxbridge candidate. He had an eclectic musical taste, and played classical guitar superbly. Developing 'pop' and modern jazz in groups.

As a child he had a voracious appetite for books and reading, which later became one of his obsessions. During his teens, he began collecting books, many of which where classics. Ben had amassed a considerable collection on diverse subjects like comparative religions, mythologies, sociology and philosophy. These esoteric topics fascinated him and he would spend hours exploring various theories to see where they led. In itself there was nothing wrong with this thirst for information. Yet he became more and more withdrawn into whatever subject matter he was currently focusing.

During his early teens, he had been introduced to cannabis by his brother and circle of friends as they played fantasy role play games, in which he used many different identities.

Ben began playing with words, using synonyms and different ways of communicating He changed the way he wrote things down in letters. It seemed at first, just another of his quirky ways of doing things. But sometime during this transition from his 'digs' in Hampshire, where he had been studying to the Halls of Residence in Lampeter, he became more disconnected with reality as he experimented with 'magic'.

He was exploring the idea of 'astral travel 'and while he lived in this make-believe world, became very isolated.

During the first semester he had become a strict 'vegan', and the arguments for this change in his diet seemed quite plausible at the time, so we respected his viewpoint. It was only later that we discovered that this about his fear of CJD 'mad cow' disease and a friendship with an animal rights activator, who seemed to dominate his thinking. Along with other fears about allergies, his food anxiety grew.

Ben was also struggling with identity and especially his sexual orientation. I remember him presenting himself for collection home from University, once, dressed in a mix of male and female clothing. We made no comment and just continued to treat Ben with respect about his personal identity. He eventually he chose to dress in male clothing. It would not have mattered what he decided, as long as he was comfortable with who he was. Many people struggle through their whole lives not able to reconcile who they truly are, or with what their family imagine they should be.

Ben may have been looking at how he could fit into an ever increasingly confusing society. He has always showed great concern and interest in the way we treat our planet.

Since the summer of 1999 he has come a long way and has worked hard to achieve a worthwhile role in society. Now with a more realistic understanding of 'who' rather than 'what' he is now.

Ben will always try to show a brighter side than he probably is actually feeling. So it is difficult for people to know when he is 'going under' again. The most likely cause of Ben deteriorating, is if he loses hope about his life moving forward or that his situation will improve. Anyone who had such plans and hopes for the future, needs encouragement, respect and opportunities to improve.

Thank you

I handed this to the MIND team who were supporting him at the time, because I felt they needed to understand Ben and where his many thought processes had led him.

We were grateful that they took time to fully understand Ben as a whole person and not just the part represented as a 'client'.

MIND do seem to have a policy of respecting the wishes of the people they come in contact with and will do all that they are able within the narrow financial constraints that rule every service these days. I am very thankful for the help and advice they have offered our son over the years.

We seemed to find ourselves in a permanent state of conflict with whatever authorities were in charge of managing Ben's care. This was not intentional on our part, but nowhere could we see that the care on offer was holistic enough to safeguard Ben from falling ill again through despair of getting the basic psychological support he needed.

Some way or another the idea manifested itself that once he was ensconced in a suitably calm environment, taking his medications regularly - however much he hated their side effects - and with a few opportunities to socialise, all would be well.

Nothing could be further from the truth. Ben wanted to be a part of the *solution* and to begin to find a way *through* his problems, not just to be doused with drugs and left dangling mid-air between small journeys of respite care - which often hindered his progress - and constant promises of talking therapy which, more often than not, was non existent or rationed.

I found a useful statement from YouTube Thursday, 2 July 2009

'R D Laing, the revolutionary doctor, discovered not too long ago that all you had to do with schizophrenics was talk to them.'

I read that over the years 'Cognitive Behaviour Therapy' has been found by doctors in three of the largest studies made in this field, to be far more effective than neuroleptic drugs and so now advances in 'Neuro Linguistic Programming' are giving an opportunity to improve lives.

I have included an extract from a letter, I sent in desperation, asking for more help for Ben. But it did not get the urgent response I needed. The mental health services, then as now, were under severe pressure and unless the person concerned was about to commit suicide or a crime, then it was probably put aside until more resources were available.

Dept. of Clinical &
Community Psychology
Church Lane, Heavitree
Exeter EX2 5SH

23rd. October 2001

Dear J M,

I am writing to you regarding our son Benjamin, who you have met through the 'Experts by Experience' group from the Joan of Arc room.

I am not too sure where to begin but I am feeling desperate and exhausted after caring for him without a break for over two and a half years.

He has received only a few sessions with a good clinical psychologist, which came to an end last autumn when the post was closed at Tiverton and the Psychologist took a new post in Plymouth. We have been paying privately for Ben to visit a Psychotherapist in Exeter.

Ben is in a very lonely position that is becoming increasingly desperate. He has taken it into his head to 'work with young people' on the streets of Uffculme. He explained that the inspiration came from the HVN group and their idea of working with young people. Rather than wait for the right support to begin a proper work he has gone out and created a group of very young teenage 'hangers-on' in the village. He has been wrongly accused by some of being a Paedophile and a drug pusher.

My husband and I have tried to explain to him the dangers of such liaisons and this has caused the most extreme family tension.

He is desperate for human contact apart from us, of his own age and intellect. He is also in great need of more psychological help than he is receiving at present.

Can you suggest someone to assist Ben's progress towards recovery. We feel that less drugs and a more cognitive form of treatment would be better. I appreciate that he is not in your 'area' and that you are a very busy man with many commitments, but I do not know who to ask any more.

Ben's CPN did arrange a placement for Ben in a Residential unit in Tiverton soon after, so this enabled us to resolve the problem that Ben was enduring in the local community. It was to be the beginning of Ben living a more independent, if rather precarious life, away from his family. But it did not address the issue of entitlement to therapeutic treatment we knew Ben was owed.

Ben had moved from Tiverton to Magdalen Street in Exeter and was in a much less stable environment, by the time a letter arrived regarding any treatment with this particular Psychologist. Nothing further happened about the NHS 'talking therapy' treatment. His CPN received a letter, in July 2002, a copy of which was sent to Ben, stating that there was a waiting list for therapy and Ben would be contacted as soon as an appointment became available.

Having not heard anything, I tried writing once more in March 2004 after waiting a considerable time, but it was all to no avail.

Dept. of Clinical & Community Psychology
Exeter EX2 5SH

Dear Mr. M,

We are wondering how far up the waiting list our son Ben is now, for an appointment with you?

He has been waiting to see you for over two years now and we are very concerned with his present state of mind.

We have had to make more private appointments for him with the therapist who previously helped Ben through a difficult patch.

We really do believe that some form of cognitive treatment would help him greatly alongside the drugs he is prescribed. At the present moment he is feeling very low and has stopped attending the Hearing Voices group that has helped him so much, because he is frightened to go out into the city.

Can you please let us know what the current situation is regarding his chances of some psychological help? We do appreciate any help he receives and value your time in reading this letter.

I have searched through the piles of correspondence I have kept, but cannot find a reply to this request. I believe Mr. M moved on to Plymouth and so we never did resolve this issue satisfactorily.

I think it was around this time, that Ben tried to take another overdose. I have no complete record in the diaries found, mainly due to our being rather involved with the situation as it was occurring. I noted he was very distressed and frightened, having been subjected to various taunts in the city including how he dressed.

I realised that we were never going to get the help needed for Ben from the NHS and so would just have to try to continue privately.

You will note that I also sent a copy to Ben's current CPN, in order to keep them informed of any treatment outside the NHS system that we were using. Thankfully, Richard Skinner was still available and accepted Ben again.

14th January 2004

Exeter

Dear Richard,

We are writing on behalf of our son Benjamin.

It has been some time since you last helped him, and we were wondering if you would consider seeing him again.

He is now living in a well organised house in Exeter run by 'MIND' support workers. He still hears voices and takes medication for his psychosis, but he has been waiting now nearly two years to see a psychologist. He still has many problems two of which seem to bother him more than others. They are obsessive thoughts and compulsive behaviour. These make his day to day life very difficult. He often makes friends with quite unsuitable people, who rather than assist him to raise his horizons, tend drag him under and then dump him.

He is still on benefits and would not be able to afford very much, but feels that he is not receiving enough help with his mental health problems and medication as you know, is not the full solution. It just masks them.

He has asked us to make the initial contact, and would be willing to meet you for a re-assessment of what you would consider to be the best way forward.

Yours Sincerely

Mr & Mrs M. Durkin

cc CPN Exeter.

Dangerousness in Mentally ill people.

A lot of negative stuff still surrounds the diagnosis of Schizophrenia. So much news and media attention has been focused on the few violent incidents that have occurred mainly due to the lack of care in the lead up to such situations.

When a sufferer of aggressive voices continually is ignored or just doused down with drugs, so that they cannot escape these voices, they become powerless to cope with their affliction. This can overwhelm the person to such an extent that the voice is all they hear and no amount of psychiatric intervention will prevent total mental melt down.

A person who has been desperately crying for help, yet dosed with ever more powerful drugs to shut them up will eventually explode like a volcano.

People need to be listened to at the outset of their distress. Then given enough time to see that whoever is involved with their care can be trusted. The response should be less about control, than assisting someone to make sense of what they are experiencing.

Inquiries in hospitals regarding staff as abusers of patients subtly changed when in 1984 a former inpatient of a mental health hospital killed her former social worker. Community care became associated thereafter with danger regarding the mentally ill. Then, in 1992 there were a group of tragic cases involving people with mental health problems who attacked and killed strangers, thus giving rise to the sense that acts of random, irrational violence were on the increase. This, however, is far from the truth.

For many years a common perception has evolved that people with mental health problems are likely to have violent outbursts, culminating in serious injury or death. This viewpoint has been greatly exaggerated in films, media and novels for dramatic purposes and has fuelled this misconception. It is far more likely that someone in mental distress will do themselves harm or commit suicide. Various reports by Home Office Crime statistics, Psychiatric Archives and Hospital Statistics have been written, which can be viewed online or in public libraries showing that out of the number of homicides in England and Wales a relatively small number in the population would have been committed by those with mental illness.

Ben was far more likely and did, indeed, suffer the effects of people's prejudice against his condition, than he would ever dream of behaving towards them. Being beaten up for looking different or even looking like someone of another race or creed is not only unpleasant, but can also take away the sense of belonging to the community.

Ben's Medications and their effects.

In the first months he had his medication changed a few times due to the horrible side effects he suffered.

To begin with Ben was given liquid medication due to him being 'vegan'. So the first medication he was prescribed - back in the late summer of 1999 - was Haloperidol.

This had the effect of weight gain and, worse than that, he began to develop enlarged breasts.

He was then given Melleril which contains the active ingredient thioridazine. Ben took this, too, in liquid form which contains 25 mg of the active ingredient. The side-effects that occurred were unpleasant: such as sweating, weight gain, blurred vision, sleep disturbances to name just a few. This belongs to a group of medicines known as the phenothiazine antipsychotics. It acts by blocking a variety of receptors in the brain, particularly dopamine receptors. Dopamine is involved in transmitting signals between brain cells. When there is an excess amount of dopamine in the brain it is believed to cause over-stimulation of dopamine receptors. These receptors normally act to modify behaviour and over-stimulation may result in psychotic illness. Thioridazine blocks these receptors and stops them becoming over-stimulated, thereby thought to help control psychotic illness. This medicine was used to treat schizophrenia but only as a second line treatment if other medicines have failed. However it has a nasty history of causing Heart arrhythmia (irregular heartbeat).

Thiroidiazine is an old style (typical) antipsychotic that was taken off the market due to its alarming propensity to cause people to drop dead from a particularly nasty ventricular arrhythmia called *Torsades de Pointes - TdP* (twisting of the points). Its use was discontinued in the UK in June 2005.

Ben was then prescribed Respiridone but felt sick immediately on taking it. Amisulpiride was then given instead this time in tablet form as he was no longer a vegan, along with an antidepressant called Citalopram (for panic attacks). Neither of these were particularly successful and his withdrawal from Citalopram felt like 'earthquakes erupting inside him all the time'.

However there was a time when he'd forgotten to take it and nothing adverse happened, but when put back on it again he suffered from compulsive overdosing.

He was also prescribed Prothiaden - known also as Dothiepin - as an antidepressant at some time, but this is a tricyclic antidepressant medicine that is used to treat patients affected by depression and anxiety: it does not relieve the voices. Drowsiness may occur as a result of taking this medicine and for this reason many doctors recommend it for patients diagnosed with anxiety disorders who are agitated and have difficulties related to sleep.

Other similar disorders may also be treated by it, and it has been studied for chronic pain disorders, nerve pain and other similar conditions. Some patients are prescribed it for migraine, to prevent headaches and other symptoms. When used for depression it is believed that the drug acts on the brain cells and helps to prolong the effects of neurotransmitters, thereby helping to relieve depression.

Resperidone (better known by its trade name Risperdal) and Clozapine also have rather nasty sided effects, especially when taken for any length of time. The withdrawal symptoms from these can be just as unpleasant as the condition they are meant to treat.

Ben cannot take any form of anti-depressant now as they tend to make him overdose accidentally when he feels they are not working. Some anti-depressants are linked to suicidal tendencies.

He was then tried on Aripiprazole for a week, another atypical antipsychotic medication but this caused severe and agonising cramps so had to be discontinued.

His most recently prescribed drug, Quetiapine, is an atypical antipsychotic. He is now on the lowest possible dose of this and finds it better to take at night time given how drowsy it makes him feel.

Although this drug does not relieve all symptoms of psychosis, the way he administers his dosage keeps his levels of anxiety and disturbance at bay during the day and allows him to sleep at night. He feels at last, that he has a certain amount of control over the drugs he is prescribed and he is now more regularly monitored for any adverse effects.

Exactly how it works is not known. It is thought to affect certain substances in the brain for use in Schizophrenia.

It is debatable whether, as a class, typical or atypical antipsychotics are more effective. Both have equal drop-out and symptom relapse rates when typicals are used at low to moderate dosages. While Quetiapine has lower rates of extrapyramidal side effects, there is greater sleepiness and rates of dry mouth.

Quetiapine should only be discontinued gradually, with careful consideration from the prescribing doctor, to avoid withdrawal symptoms or relapse.

All this information is so complicated and often shrouded in medical jargon that anyone trying to fathom out how to negotiate with their doctor what dosage works for them can feel that they are stepping into a minefield!

Because of the worry about the effects that long term use of all forms of antipsychotic medication would have, I purchased a book called 'Toxic Psychiatry' by Peter Breggin quite early in our experience which gave clear evidence of the long term problems associated with taking neuroleptics and how the use of less toxic and alternative methods could be found.

This book became an essential tool in our understanding the uses and the strength of many medications Ben was prescribed. It also helped me to keep watch in case of possible side effects that might later result in permanent damage. I must state here though, that this book is not suitable to use as a treatment handbook. It has a very clear warning at the beginning about stopping one's medication without medical advice. Very serious, sometimes fatal, consequences can arise from the misuse of some psychiatric drugs.

I hope that by being fairly frank about the list of medications Ben has been prescribed over a number of years that you will see we are not *against* the use of drugs, but are wary of being forced to take something that could be the cause of other health problems.

It is wise if possible, to obtain as much information about the medication being offered before accepting it, as it is harder to come off many of them once the dosage has begun.

Ben still hears his voices. None of these medications has stopped this phenomena. Some have even made it harder to control the negative side of voice hearing and leave him feeling totally unable to cope because of an inability to escape a frightening mental 'fog' while plagued by vicious voices.

It is far better if he can set aside some space and time to cope with his voices in his own way. This is something that has had to be learned from others who have experienced similar things.

Many of the medical procedures followed for mentally distressed people can still be quite alarming. But also today there is a much more open attitude to treatment, where the 'patient' or 'client' is given opportunities to discuss and question what is suggested.

Hopefully today you will find a better response to your needs, whether 'client' or carer. I have tried to show that it is often when the channels of communication break down between the various people involved, that problems arise. That is why keeping notes, however brief, are very helpful when having to negotiate on several levels.

10

Not so much Recovery as 'Transformation'

Early during those first months of severe psychosis Ben told me of his visitation from an angel-type being which told him that he would be 'Transformed'. According to Ben it was explained to him that this process would be long and arduous and not the same as is understood by 'recovery'.

This 'transformation' would therefore change who he was at the time of his *Illth* into someone who had been given enlightenment regarding the process of his seeming madness. He became an expert by experience; in the true sense.

A visit to an Intervoice Meeting of HVN in Maastricht in 2002 was to have a significant effect on Ben. Although quite unwell still, he was to take the journey with the help of someone at the Joan of Arc room, called Claire. Ben was able to have a discussion with Rufus May and Professor Marius Romme. It was a very stimulating time, giving Ben more insight for future research into voice hearing, but because of his state of mind then, he does not now remember much more about his time there.

Now several years have passed and many more changes have taken place.

Ben has worked with me on this book, which has been good for both of us. Many memories, not all pleasant, came flooding back and some needed careful handling. But it is encouraging that Ben is now able to be more involved. He has travelled this journey now for a long while and views the horizon with more hope.

Because his story will continue long after this is published it is not easy to know how to complete what I need to say to you.

Yet I can imagine that starting out on such a journey, whether with a supportive family or on your own, you may have been able to connect in some way with our experiences and not feel so alone.

I hope that you and those who care for you find the support and encouragement you need to travel at your own speed; towards a future in which perhaps you once felt impossible to believe.

There are some useful books, addresses and contacts at the end of this book which are current to the time of writing.

The Open Dialogue and Soteria House models of care, as well as Hearing Voices Network and The Bridge Collective C. I. C. in this-area have all played important parts in our continuing journey.

Maybe also, by the time you read this, even more groups and methods will have emerged that can help, encourage and empower you to become more confident and fulfilled. Hopefully they will be available where you live. Everyone's experience is unique.

In conclusion, I can say that we had hoped for a happier course for Ben's life with a career of his choice and possibly a degree or two by now. Yet we are very proud of his achievements as he has moved forward in a creative way to assist others to find answers and even question their own diagnosis and treatment.

We have survived as a family having experienced many ups and downs and are much closer to understanding how the mind can alter under severe stress, changing lives, and changing futures.

So we do urge you to seek as much help from as many places as you can, in order to find what is right for you.

I am so thankful that Ben has felt able to contribute to this book himself. He has, over the years, made sufficient progress to give talks about the things that have happened to him and how he has struggled to overcome them, often with only his family's support. He wants to be more involved with becoming part of the solution. Offering others hope and guidance, whether they are the professionals or those on the receiving end of 'treatment'.

Of course he still needs more support than is being offered, to help him organise his daily routines. That aspect of his life will always be a struggle.

Just recently Ben had his MIND care support worker removed, due to budget cuts and the fact he is not deemed to be currently 'at risk'.

This is not the best way to avoid his future needs becoming critical again. It may be that the poor financial management of resources for the Mental Health part of the NHS sees money supposed to be allocated to them, 'syphoned off' to more 'urgent' departments. What ever the cause of the critical state of this area of treatment, serious problems have arisen with reduced staffing levels. Those working in this sector can feel undervalued, overworked and in serious danger of needing the very services that they are expected to provide. The stress levels of most NHS staff at every grade are now acute. A dangerous state of affairs could occur in which, not only a 'patient' needing care, but a provider needing support, could see the system collapse.

Uncertainty of one's future whether in employment or reliant on social care and housing is exacerbating the conditions of many people who are desperate for the kind of care we gave our son.

It is not 'rocket science' to arrange for groups of lay people willing to befriend and become supporters of those with various mental health needs. The Soteria House idea of peer support and people meeting and taking time to listen; making meals, sharing everyday tasks, could be adapted perhaps to a day or evening situation similar to that of the now popular Dementia Cafes.

So much 'day care' has closed due to funding shortages or staffing levels needing to comply with stringent health and safety regulations, that those who once had havens of enjoyment and safety to visit, are now dangerously isolated in homes which are often unsuitable or depressing to live in.

At the time of my writing these last few pages, Ben is not managing quite so well and has had to stop giving his talks for a while. He is plagued again by voices telling him he cannot go out and enjoy himself, as he is not good enough. He fears getting a public panic attack which is not only very embarrassing but can be dangerous. If he is trying to walk along a busy street or near a railway platform the urge to throw himself outward and into oncoming transport can be overwhelming when in this heightened state of anxiety.

As for this talk of 'care in the community' a lot of what I have seen for the mentally ill is next to 'no care' and very little 'community'. Small desperately underfunded groups such as The Bridge

Collective are now having to cope with ever more desperate people needing help.

The problem I see today is that any property costs so much to buy and maintain that administration costs, along with health and safety regulations overriding any budget plan, ensure that such places of safety and respite are virtually non-existent. Perhaps the best way forward is using social media and other networking methods to gather interested, trustworthy people together to form small cells of support to those who have slipped through the 'care net' due to cuts. These could just offer transport to someone unable to get to an appointment due to a panic attack, or being with someone as they do a weekly shop, or visit the doctor. It may be that another person may just need someone to remind them to take their medication and prepare a meal. All these small everyday things can become a huge problem when faced with hallucinations or auditory interference.

Much of what is on offer during a crisis, if you are lucky enough to be offered a place in a hospital, is a very clinical and unwelcoming room, where the vulnerable person is expected to wait to be 'treated'. The lighting is often too bright and there is no soft sofa for someone to just cling on to while they are being questioned about how they feel and what they might have done. The atmosphere of many such places has no visual focus point, like a calming fish tank, or pleasant view. They are just not homely.

Should a person have the unfortunate experience of being forced into a Police cell first then this just adds to their fear and confusion.

How is it that in this modern day world we have so little regard still for those in mental torment?

I return then to Ben, who I hope will regain the confidence that he felt when he wrote the final paragraphs of this book some months ago.

Despite the loss of much of his memory both long and short term, he tries to work through ideas for improving 'the system' in which care has been patchy but is now almost non existent.

Sadly, due to the constant drugs prescribed over many years, he can no longer remember how to play the guitar. His playing was a delight to me all those years ago. Often I would think it was coming from the radio, not realising it was him playing a lovely classical piece. I wish I had some recordings but think they may never have existed. He still has an eclectic taste in music. He reads, but confines this only what he feels is beneficial. Too much information gathered can adversely affect him.

He does now have a feline companion, called Lola. She is an oversized ball of longhaired 'tabbiness' who inhabits both his waking and sleeping hours. Totally reliant on Ben for her survival as a nervous 'house 'cat, she offers that soft encouragement needed each day to kick start him into the mundane responsibilities of caring for another dependant life. Lola is non-judgemental and so completely devoid of the woes associated with guilt. So Ben can tell her anything he likes knowing she will keep it to herself.

This new flatmate has given Ben the kind of company he never found with so many humans; that of complete trust.

Ben is quite literally, central to this book. His poems, stories, pictures all show how creative a thinker he has always been.

I shall let Ben have the final word.

> I volunteer my time as a member of a peer support group community called The Bridge Collective C. I. C. in Exeter. In the course of this volunteering I contribute to a number of groups within this Collective.
>
> I was a founder of the 'Underground Sounds' which provides a space for people to create and record music (or just drink coffee and natter) in a relaxed, open atmosphere.
>
> I was not the right person to develop it further, but once it had become securely established, I happily passed on the baton to those who could and would.
>
> I have been an active member of 'Experts by Experience' for the last nine years. In this role I contribute insights into psychosis, schizophrenia and the philosophical questions they have raised, to diverse audiences of health practitioners in training. I regularly give talks to trainee doctors (in their second and third year of study) Psychological students in their final year before qualifying as Clinical Psychiatrists and contribute to a well regarded module in the training of psychiatric nurses.
>
> I do this without pay, for the express purpose of changing the culture of mental health services and providing an honest and hopeful glimpse into a complex experience.

I also co host a monthly peer support group within the Bridge Collective called 'Open Minds'

It provides the opportunity for those with experiences that might be classified as psychotic, to discuss their experiences frankly and openly with each other, comparing notes and sharing techniques and strategies for maintaining wellbeingI also contribute my time to the regular Open Days, where I view myself as a 'point of contact' whereby certain conversations may happen.

I have made myself available to contribute to research on community development as and when opportunities have arisen.

I anticipate this to be a lengthy commitment, but one cannot predict the future.

Bibliography and Contacts

(The contacts information and addresses are correct at time of publication.)

Bibliography

Toxic Psychiatry - *Peter Breggin*

Living with Voices, 50 Stories of Recovery - *Prof Marius Romme, Dr Sandra Escher, Jacqui Dillon, Dr. Dirk Corstens, Prof Mervyn Morris*

Raising our Voices - An account of the Hearing Voices Movement *James Adams*

Working to Recovery - *Karen Taylor, Ron Coleman & Paul Baker*

Working with Voices II: Victim to Victor - *Workbook first published in 1997 - Ron Coleman & Mike Smith*

Soteria Through Madness to Deliverance - *Loren Mosher,* **Voyce Hendrix** *with Deborah C. Fort*

Paper Boats - *Mary E. Gould*

Useful Contacts

Hearing Voices Network HVN: *For people who hear voices, see visions or have any other forms of unusual perceptions.*

Working to Recovery Ltd. Mental Health Recovery. *Ron Coleman & Karen Taylor*

MIND: Mind for better mental health - *Advice and support and respect to empower anyone experiencing a mental health problem.*

Open Dialogue: *An International Community with resources and training courses to aid recovery from many Mental Health conditions*

Soteria Network: *Promoting the development of drug free and minimum medication therapeutic environments for people experiencing psychosis.*